The Artist's Life

This book delves into the lives, growth, and inner workings of creative artists, sharing stories about the lives of those who have built their career in the arts. Drawing from interviews with more than 60 expert artists from varied domains – including Oscar, Grammy, Emmy, and Pulitzer Prize winners – these detailed, intimate, and often surprising anecdotes shed light on creativity from both personal and professional perspectives. Chapters focus on the influences of family and school on creativity, through early discoveries and passions that led to growth and development. In their own words, interviewees describe the joys of "making it" in the creative world alongside the realities of the business, from finances to relationships and possible legacies. Taking a narrative approach that reveals the hidden truths about being a creative artist, this book offers a rare window on creativity for researchers and artists alike.

BETH LEIBSON is a writer and editor for the Mount Sinai Health System. She is the author of three books: *The Cancer Survivor Handbook* (2014), *Good Clean Food* (2013), and *I'm Too Young to Have Breast Cancer* (2004), which received an award from the Susan G Komen foundation.

JAMES C. KAUFMAN is a professor of educational psychology at the Neag School of Education at the University of Connecticut. He has written or edited more than 50 books, including *The Creativity Advantage* (2023). He has won many awards from such places as APA, NAGC, and Mensa.

The Artist's Life

The Heartbeat of the Creative Person

BETH LEIBSON

JAMES C. KAUFMAN
University of Connecticut

CAMBRIDGE
UNIVERSITY PRESS

![Cambridge University Press logo] **CAMBRIDGE**
UNIVERSITY PRESS

Shaftesbury Road, Cambridge CB2 8EA, United Kingdom

One Liberty Plaza, 20th Floor, New York, NY 10006, USA

477 Williamstown Road, Port Melbourne, VIC 3207, Australia

314–321, 3rd Floor, Plot 3, Splendor Forum, Jasola District Centre,
New Delhi – 110025, India

103 Penang Road, #05–06/07, Visioncrest Commercial, Singapore 238467

Cambridge University Press is part of Cambridge University Press & Assessment,
a department of the University of Cambridge.

We share the University's mission to contribute to society through the pursuit of
education, learning and research at the highest international levels of excellence.

www.cambridge.org
Information on this title: www.cambridge.org/9781009625999

DOI: 10.1017/9781009626026

© Beth Leibson and James C. Kaufman 2026

When citing this work, please include a reference to the DOI 10.1017/9781009626026

First published 2026

Front cover: 'Windows on the World' by Matteo Pericoli. Copyright (c) 2014 by Matteo
Pericoli, used by permission of The Wylie Agency LLC.

A catalogue record for this publication is available from the British Library

*A Cataloging-in-Publication data record for this book is available from the Library of
Congress.*

ISBN 978-1-009-62599-9 Hardback
ISBN 978-1-009-62603-3 Paperback

For EU product safety concerns, contact us at Calle de José Abascal,
56, 1°, 28003 Madrid, Spain, or email eugpsr@cambridge.org

For Maya and Ari.
Surprise – you thought this would never happen!
With all my love

                                   – Beth

For my boys, Jacob and Asher.
With all of my love, forever
                          – James

Contents

Interviewees

Diana Abu-Jaber is a novelist and memoirist. Her novel *Crescent* won the PEN Center Award for Literary Fiction and the American Book Award; *Birds of Paradise* won the Arab American National Book Award. Her most recent novel, *Fencing with the King*, was named one of *The Washington Post*'s best books of the year.

Piers Anthony is the author of more than 200 fantasy and science fiction novels, including 21 *New York Times* bestsellers. He may be best known for the Xanth series, which has 50 volumes, beginning with *A Spell for Chameleon*, and includes titles starting with every letter of the alphabet. He has also written historical fiction, horror, and an autobiography, *Bio of An Ogre*. He has won the British Fantasy Award, the Phoenix Award, and four Hugo nominations.

Chris Bearde was a TV comedy writer, director, and producer. He created and produced *The Gong Show* and *The Sonny and Cher Comedy Hour* and produced many other shows, including *That's My Mama*. He received nine Emmy nominations, winning for his work as senior writer on *Rowan & Martin's Laugh In*. He was also the creator of the ahead-of-its-time Showtime cult comedy classic *Sherman Oaks*. Bearde helped write and produce numerous television specials for many legends, perhaps most notably co-writing Elvis Presley's 1968 comeback special. Bearde died on April 23, 2017.

T. Coraghessan Boyle has written 19 novels and 12 collections of short stories. He has won many literary awards, including the PEN/Faulkner Award (for *World's End*), five O. Henry awards, the Bernard Malamud Prize, and the Prix Médicis Étranger. Boyle's books regularly make both the *New York Times*' bestseller and editor's choice lists. Both *Budding Prospects* and *The Road to Wellville* were filmed (the latter starring Anthony Hopkins). Boyle founded the creative writing program at the University of Southern California (USC), where he taught for decades.

John Patrick Bray is a playwright and independent screenwriter whose plays regularly appear off-off-Broadway and all around the United States. An Associate Professor at the University of Georgia, he is the author of a textbook, *Inciting Incidents,* and he has edited or co-edited several volumes of plays for Applause Theatre and Cinema Books (including *The Best American Short Plays 2018–2019* and *Stage It and Stream It: Plays for Virtual Theater*). His plays are published with Next Stage Press, Original Works Publishing, Heartland Plays, and Off the Wall Plays, anthologized in many annual best-of collections, and have appeared in several journals. He co-wrote the Broadcast Education Association (BEA) Award-Winning feature film *Liner Notes* (Official Selection: Woodstock Film Festival) directed by his twin brother Gregg, and he wrote the shorts *Escapism* (also a BEA Award-Winner) and *Barflies.*

Susan Breen is the award-winning author of *The Fiction Class* and the Maggie Dove mystery series. Her short stories have been published in *Alfred Hitchcock's Mystery Magazine, Ellery Queen Mystery Magazine,* and, most recently, the Anthony-award winning MWA anthology, *Crime Hits Home.* Breen teaches novel writing at Gotham Writers and is on the staff of the New York Write to Pitch Workshop.

Aviva Briefel is a writer and editor of five books and many articles, on topics ranging from horror movies to Victorian literature. Her books include *Horror after 9/11: World of Fear, Cinema of Terror,* and *Labors of Fear: The Modern Horror Film Goes to Work.* She is the Edward Little Professor of the English Language and Literature and Cinema Studies at Bowdoin College.

Lisa Brody worked at Creativity for Kids/Faber-Castell USA for more than 20 years, primarily in public relations and marketing, with a focus on highlighting the importance of childhood creativity and the value of lifelong creative expression. She partnered with local and national media contacts to promote the company's extensive line of arts and craft kits for children, art supplies for children and professional artists, and premium fine-writing instruments.

Phyllis Brody co-founded Creativity for Kids, a brand of activity kits designed to stimulate children's creativity, in 1976. Her company, which was acquired by Faber-Castell, has won dozens of awards from Parents' Choice, Learning Express, Family Fun, and many others. Brody won the Lifetime Achievement Award from the American Specialty Toy Retailing Association and a Corporate Citizenship Award from President Clinton, among others. After retiring, she has continued to experiment, create, and exhibit and sell her artwork.

Isabelle Bryer is a French multimedia artist living in Los Angeles. She paints mainly acrylic on canvas and watercolor. She recently created a collection of art stickers. Bryer is also program director and art instructor in an eating disorder recovery program. Born near Lyon, France, she worked in fashion design in France and New York City before moving to California.

Robert Olen Butler is a Pulitzer Prize-winning novelist who has published more than twenty novels and short story collections, including *A Good Scent from a Strange Mountain*. A winner of a Guggenheim Fellowship and National Endowment of the Arts grant, Butler judges the annual Robert Olen Butler Prize for short fiction. He is a distinguished professor at Florida State University; his master classes on creative writing have been compiled into the book *From Where You Dream*.

Cecil Castellucci is the award-winning and *New York Times* bestselling author of books and graphic novels for young adults. They have written *Batgirl* for DC Comics, in addition to other graphic novels. They have written three opera librettos, and are the former Children's Correspondence Coordinator for *The Rumpus*, a two-time MacDowell Fellow, and the founding YA Editor at the *LA Review of Books*.

Donna Lynne Champlin is an OBIE, Drama Desk, and Gracie award-winning actress best known as Paula Proctor on the Emmy award-winning *Crazy Ex-Girlfriend*. Other TV/film credits include *Feel the Beat, The First Lady*, and *The Perfect Couple*. Broadway credits include *James Joyce's The Dead, By Jeeves, Hollywood Arms, Billy Elliot*, and *Sweeney Todd* (in which she played the accordion, flute, and piano as Pirelli). In 2009, she sang, arranged the music, and played all the instruments for her acclaimed solo album *Old Friends*, which she recorded in her bathroom and self-produced on a $1,000 budget.

Susan Choi is the author of six novels, including *Trust Exercise*, which received the 2019 National Book Award for fiction. She has also been a recipient of the Asian American Literary Award for fiction, the PEN/ W. G. Sebald Award, a Lamba Literary award, the 2021 *Sunday Times* Audible Short Story Award, and fellowships from the National Endowment for the Arts and the Guggenheim Foundation. She serves as a trustee of PEN America and teaches in The Writing Seminars at Johns Hopkins University.

Michael Colby is a librettist, lyricist, and author. His musical *Charlotte Sweet* was nominated for a Drama Desk Award. His other musicals include *Tales of Tinseltown*, *North Atlantic*, *Slay it with Music*, and a collection of story songs, *Other Lives*. Colby also wrote a memoir, *The Algonquin Kid*.

Greg DeLiso is an indie director, producer, editor, writer, and actor who co-wrote and directed *Hectic Knife*. He also directed the documentary *Canada's Best Kept Secret*.

Kristoffer Diaz is a playwright, librettist, screenwriter, and educator. His play *The Elaborate Entrance of Chad Deity* was a finalist for the Pulitzer Prize in Drama. His musical *Hell's Kitchen* (created with Alicia Keys) premiered on Broadway in Spring 2024 and was nominated for thirteen Tony Awards, including Best Book. Other full-length titles include *Welcome to Arroyo's, Reggie Hoops, Hercules*, and *The Unfortunates*. His work has been produced, commissioned, and developed at The Public Theater, Dallas Theater Center, Geffen Playhouse, ACT, Center Theatre Group, The Goodman, Second Stage, Victory Gardens, and Oregon Shakespeare Festival, among many others. Awards include the Guggenheim, Jerome, Van Lier, NYFA, and Gail Merrifield Papp Fellowships; *New York Times* Outstanding Playwright Award; Lucille Lortel, Equity Jeff, and OBIE Awards; and the Future Aesthetics Artist Regrant, among others. As a screenwriter, Kristoffer has developed original television pilots for HBO and FX, written for the first season of Netflix's *GLOW*, and adapted the musical *Rent* for FOX. Diaz teaches playwriting at New York University. He is an alumnus of New

Dramatists and a member of its Board of Directors, and the current secretary of the Dramatists Guild Council.

Shanee Epstein is an award-winning painter who co-founded the 440 Gallery in Park Slope, Brooklyn. She received her MFA at Pratt Institute and specializes in collages and geometric paintings. Epstein returned to Western Massachusetts, after three decades in New York City, and now splits her time between Deerfield, MA and Yaffo, Israel. She works with spatial give and take, the shifting between the simple and the complex, the narrative and the abstract, and the geometry of shape with the sensuality of color and texture. Epstein is deeply connected to materiality and reusing her art. Her collages use handmade paper and fragments of earlier work. By juxtaposing old and current work, her collages are a visual autobiography.

Greg Friedler was a photographer best known for his "Naked" series, captured in several books (*Naked New York, Naked Los Angeles, Naked Las Vegas,* and *Naked London*). These works were also the subject of two documentaries. His photographs have been anthologized and exhibited all around the world. Friedler died on February 2, 2015, at the age of 44. The Greg Friedler Fund for Creative Expression was established to carry on his legacy.

Cristina García is the author of eight novels, including the National Book Award-nominated *Dreaming in Cuban* and, most recently, *Vanishing Maps*. She won the Janet Heidinger Kafka Prize and the Whiting Writer's Award, among others. García's other works include two books for young readers, a young adult novel, a volume of poetry, two Latinx anthologies, and several plays.

Tess Gerritsen is an internationally bestselling novelist who has won both the Nero Wolfe Award (for *Vanish*) and the Rita Award (for *The Surgeon*). Her series of novels featuring homicide detective Jane Rizzoli and medical examiner Maura Isles inspired the hit TNT television series *Rizzoli & Isles,* starring Angie Harmon and Sasha Alexander. Together with her son Josh Gerritsen, she has made two films: a feature-length documentary, *Magnificent Beast,* about the ancient origins of the pig taboo, and *Island Zero,* a feature-length horror movie that was released in 2018.

Maurice Godin has been acting in theater, television, and film for fifty years. His theater work runs the gamut of modern, classical, and musical plays, from the Stratford Festival to Broadway. His film and television work includes hundreds of productions, both internationally and in Hollywood. He has garnered awards and nominations, as well as national and international praise for his acting work. He began teaching and directing at California State University-Northridge in 2008 and is still teaching acting. Godin has directed dozens of operas. He continues to act, direct, write, and teach in Canada, the United States, and elsewhere.

Julie Gold is a New York-based singer-songwriter best known for Bette Midler's version of her song "From a Distance," which won the Grammy for Song of the Year in 1991. She has produced five CDs: *Dream Loud, Try Love, The Girl I Found, Love is Love is Love*, and *Sixty*. In addition, she served on the Board of Governors for the National Academy for the Recording Arts and Sciences, was a guest artist for Lincoln Center's prestigious Meet the Artist Series, and has written songs for Oxford University Press for a series that teaches English to elementary school children all over the world.

Dr. Gordon Goodman is a veteran professional actor, singer, com-poser, visual artist, and American media and entertainment psycholo-gist. He has written books and plays; directed and produced audio dramas, audiobooks, animation projects, and live industrial shows; produced TV pilots; performed internationally as a baritone soloist with symphony orchestras; was the first live-action Aquaman (DC Comics); and has his own animatronic character at a major Disney amusement park.

David Guinn is a noted muralist whose work has appeared all around the world and has been recognized by the *New York Times, Wall Street Journal*, and many other media outlets. He has won several fellowships and awards, and his paintings are displayed in numerous museums and galleries.

Doub Hanshaw is the Chief Creative Director at Free People and FP Movement. She leads a team of artists and designers.

Ann Harada created the role of Christmas Eve in the original Broadway and West End casts of *Avenue Q*, winning a special achievement award from the Outer Circle Critics. She also appeared in the original Broadway casts of *Seussical, Cinderella*, and *9 to 5*, as well as the revivals of *Into the Woods* and *Les Misérables*. Harada appeared regularly on NBC's *Smash* and was a series regular on AppleTV's *Schmigadoon*, playing both the gentle mayor's wife and the fierce Madam Frau.

Dara Horn's first two novels (*In the Image* and *The World to Come*) each won the National Jewish Book Award, and her book of essays, *People Love Dead Jews,* won her a third. Granta named her one of their Best Young American Novelists; her other awards include the Harold U. Ribalow Award, and the Reform Judaism Fiction Prize. She has written five novels.

Jacob Hyman began drumming at age 9 and eventually played the drums and sang in the Queens, NY band, Freelance Whales. Over the course of five years, Freelance Whales released two albums and played hundreds of shows and dozens of festivals in the United States, Canada, the UK, and Europe. Their songs were used in commercials (Chevy, Starbucks, and Shock Top, among others) and television shows, such as *Grey's Anatomy*. Hyman is now an oncology social worker, living in Colorado with his family.

Samantha Jakus went from cheerleading to singing to finding dance as her home. She toured for several years as a dancer with STREB Extreme Action Company. During her tenure with the company, she appeared in many films, television shows, and magazines. Jakus performed around the world, from the Pan American Games to Just for Laughs to the Metropolitan Museum of Art. She is now a creative arts therapist at The Renfrew Center of Philadelphia, specializing in movement and dance therapy.

Doug Jones is an American actor, contortionist, and mime artist, best known for portraying non-human creatures. He has been in *Mimic, Hellboy, Pan's Labyrinth, Hellboy II: The Golden Army, Crimson Peak*, and the Academy Award-winning *The Shape of Water*.

Bruce Kimmel has appeared on such classic TV shows as *Happy Days* and *M*A*S*H*. He also wrote and co-directed the cult classic *The First Nudie Musical* and other films, before becoming a Grammy-nominated record producer of more than 180 albums. In addition, Kimmel has composed songs, written and directed several other musicals, hosted monthly cabaret shows, and written twenty-five books – twenty-one novels and four memoirs.

Tine Kindermann has a dual career as a visual artist and a musician. Her paintings, tableaux and dioramas, videos, and sculptures have been shown at many galleries, art fairs, museums, theaters, and festivals in New York and Berlin. She is also a singer, has released an album of German folk songs, and has recorded with the quintet Villa Delirium. She also plays the musical saw.

Michael Kostroff played lawyer Maury Levy on the classic television series *The Wire,* and has guest-starred on more than seventy-five television shows, from *The West Wing* to *The Blacklist* to *Law & Order: SVU*. He has toured the country in *Les Misérables* and *The Producers,* wrote a regular column for *Backstage,* and authored four books for actors, including *The Stage Actor's Handbook: Traditions, Protocols, and Etiquette for the Working and Aspiring Professional.*

Michael Krass is a costume designer with twenty-four Broadway credits. He has been nominated for four Tony Awards for costume design – for *Noises Off, Machinal, The Constant Wife,* and the smash hit musical *Hadestown.* He has received three Drama Desk nominations, two Jefferson nominations, and an IRNE award. Krass has taught at New York University and Brown University.

Annie Lanzillotto is an author, poet, songwriter, and performance artist, born in the Bronx. Her books include: *Whaddyacall the Wind?, Hard Candy,* and *Pitch Roll Yaw, Schistsong,* and *L is for Lion: An Italian Bronx butch freedom memoir* (finalist for the Lambda Literary Foundation Award). Lanzillotto has toured her stage and literary work through Ireland and Italy. She has received grants from the Rockefeller Foundation, Franklin Furnace, Dixon Place, The Puffin Foundation, Creatives Rebuild New York, Trickle Up, and New York Foundation for the Arts. Her websites are AnnieLanzillotto.com and StreetCryInc.org.

Chang-rae Lee has written six novels. *The Surrendered* was a finalist for the Pulitzer Prize. His works have won numerous awards and citations, including the Hemingway Foundation/PEN Award, the American Book Award, the Anisfield-Wolf Literary Award, the Gustavus Myers Outstanding Book Award, and the Dayton Literary Peace Prize. He has taught at Princeton University and South Korea's Yonsei University, and is the Ward W. and Priscilla B. Woods Professor in the Department of English at Stanford University.

Peter Litvin is a multi-instrumentalist, composer, songwriter, producer, actor, and filmmaker. He has recorded and released more than twenty solo albums and EPs, as well as countless music videos and short films. His hired productions have amassed more than a half a billion YouTube views, and he co-wrote, produced, scored, and starred in Troma Entertainment's feature-length B-horror-comedy *Hectic Knife*. In addition to writing and recording his own music, Litvin has produced more than 1,000 songs for other artists, including many well-known YouTube personalities, as well as the full-length records *Code Cracker* (2010) and *President of Mozambique* (2012).

Bruce Mack aka **B-Mack** is a bandleader, vocalist, and multi-instrumentalist. He has conducted, toured, and recorded with many groups, such as Maya Azucena, Eighty-pound Pug, and Burnt Sugar the Arkestra Chamber, with which he recorded more than a dozen albums. Aside from those contributions, he leads and composes for his own bands, B-MACK, Rules of Aquah, the original PBR StreetGang, and Tricky Dilemma. In 2001, he began experimenting with different styles of music for each project, resulting in two full-length albums, including a solo album of his original songs, *Lo-Fi Exploits of A Misplant On Shaolin* (2018), and several critically acclaimed singles, including *Silent Witness*, in 2024. Mack is a former president of the Black Rock Coalition. The documentary *When Fried Eggs Fly* (by Constantine Limperis) is about Mack's style of teaching music during the period of his 24-year residency at PS-3 in New York City.

Lex Marie is a multidisciplinary artist whose practice encompasses paintings, sculptures, and installations that delve into personal experiences while resonating with the broader African diaspora. Marie's work has been featured in several notable group exhibitions, including

Stories from My Childhood at the Northern Illinois University Art Museum, the Cumberland Valley Juried Exhibition at the Washington County Museum of Fine Arts, *Future Places* at the Susquehanna Art Museum, and *Rooted in Voyage* at Band of Vices. She has participated in residencies at the Museum of Contemporary Art Arlington and Artist Mother Studio x Red Dirt, and has received numerous awards and grants, including the S&R Evermay Washington Award and the District of Columbia Arts and Humanities Art Bank Grant.

Country Joe McDonald released more than thirty albums as a solo artist and another fifteen as the lead singer and co-founder of Country Joe and the Fish. The psychedelic rock band played at the original Woodstock and many other classic venues. Their "I Feel Like I'm Fixing To Die Rag" is considered a classic of the counterculture era.

Geoff Meed has worked in a variety of roles over a Hollywood career that has spanned five decades, from stuntman to actor to writer to director. Meed has appeared in a range of movies and television shows, including the Oscar-winning movie *Little Miss Sunshine*, and hit shows such as *Chicago PD, S.W.A.T.*, and *Buffy the Vampire Slayer*. He has written and directed four movies, including *DC Down*, and written an additional fifteen films, including *Butch Cassidy and the Wild Bunch*. An expert martial artist, Meed also teaches private self-protection.

David Morrell's claim to international fame rests on creating the iconic character of Rambo in *First Blood*. He has written several dozen books, including the Thomas De Quincey Victorian mysteries and the spy trilogy *The Brotherhood of the Rose*, which was adapted into the only miniseries to be broadcast after a Super Bowl. Morrell co-founded the International Thriller Writers organization and has won three Bram Stoker Awards as well as the Nero, Macavity, Comic-Con Inkpot, and Bouchercon Lifetime Achievement awards. He was a tenured professor of English at the University of Iowa for sixteen years.

Gina B. Nahai is a bestselling author, columnist, and emeritus professor of Creative Writing at the University of Southern California (USC). Her five novels have been translated into eighteen languages, and have been finalists for the Orange Award, the IMPAC Award, the Harold J. Ribalow Award, and the Jewish Book Council's Fiction Award. She is the winner of the Los Angeles Arts Council Award, the Persian Heritage Foundation's Award, The Simon Rockower Award, and the Phi Kappa Phi Award.

Marianna Mott Newirth is a librettist, playwright, and creative producer. Previously an Emmy-nominated maker of broadcast TV documentaries and video producer, she now devotes her time to writing libretti, plays, and short stories while also serving as executive producer and co-founder of New York City's first disability-affirmative opera company, Opera Praktikos.

Steven Okazaki won an Academy Award, along with four Oscar nominations, a Primetime Emmy (for HBO's *White Light/Black Rain: The Destruction of Hiroshima and Nagasaki*), two UNESCO awards, and two Sundance Grand Jury Prize nominations. His short film *Days of Waiting* earned him both an Oscar and a Peabody Award. He is married to *New York Times* bestselling author and journalist Peggy Orenstein.

Peggy Orenstein is a journalist and the *New York Times* bestselling author of eight nonfiction books, including *Boys & Sex, Girls & Sex*, and *Unraveling*, a book about craft and creativity. She is a regular contributor to the *New York Times Magazine* and many other national publications. Orenstein was named one of "40 women who changed the media business in the past 40 years" by the *Columbia Journalism Review*. Her husband, Steven Okazaki, is an Oscar-winning documentary filmmaker.

Jim Piddock has been an actor, writer, and producer for nearly half a century, and is probably best known for his roles in the classic Christopher Guest comedies, such as *Best in Show, A Mighty Wind*, and *Mascots*. He has appeared in many other films, including *Lethal Weapon 2, Independence Day*, and *The Prestige*, and been in about 100 television shows, including *Modern Family, Friends*, and *Lost*. As a writer, his credits include the hit comedy film *Tooth Fairy* and the HBO series *Family Tree*. Piddock was also in the original Broadway cast of *Noises Off* and, more recently, wrote a memoir titled *Caught with My Pants Down and Other Tales from a Life in Hollywood*.

Deborah Pratt was the co-creator, executive producer, and head writer of the classic science fiction series *Quantum Leap*, in which she also served as the narrator and played Ziggy. She returned as the executive producer and director of the recent *Quantum Leap* revival. Pratt was nominated for three Emmys for her work on the original series and received a fourth nomination for writing *Our Friend, Martin*. She has also acted in numerous films and television shows and she wrote the Vision Quest book series and spin-off graphic novel *Warrior One*.

Steve Riffkin has had an eclectic career in music and theater. He performed and composed music for *Kids' Writes*, a children's program on Nickelodeon, in the 1980s. Riffkin was also the Artistic Director of Peace Child International, which led exchange programs for children with other countries, perhaps most notably the former Soviet Union. His music arrangements have been played around the world by the Kronos String Quartet and The Brass Band, at the BBC, and used in a Charlie Brown special. Riffkin led the performing arts program at Marin Country Day School for many years.

Mary Roach is the author of the *New York Times* bestsellers *Stiff*, *Spook*, *Bonk*, *Gulp*, *Grunt*, *Fuzz*, and *Packing for Mars*. She has written for *National Geographic*, *Wired*, and *The New York Times Magazine*, among others, and her TED talk made the TED 20 Most Watched list. She has been a guest editor for *Best American Science and Nature Writing* and a finalist for the Royal Society's Winton Prize.

J. Cleary Rubinos is an arts administrator based in Philadelphia who, at one point, specialized in wedding and portrait photography. Rubinos has worked for arts collectives, cabarets, storytelling workshops, and architectural design firms.

Bill Russell was nominated for two Tony awards for his 1997 Broadway musical *Side Show*, and its 2014 revival was nominated for Best Revival by the Outer Critics Circle. He has directed his musicals *Pageant* and *Elegies for Angels, Punks, and Raging Queens* in London's West End, and *Elegies* was filmed with an all-star cast for World AIDS Day. He also wrote the off-Broadway musicals *Fourtune*, *The Last Smoker in America*, and *Unexpected Joy*. His song "Take the Flame" is the official anthem of the Gay Games.

Dana Sachs is a novelist, journalist, and translator. She has published two novels, *If You Lived Here* and *The Secret of the Nightingale Palace,* and three books of nonfiction, including her most recent, *All Else Failed: The Unlikely Volunteers at the Heart of the Migrant Aid Crisis.* Sachs also made a documentary with her sister, *Which Way is East,* and cofounded the nonprofit Humanity Now: Direct Refugee Relief.

Rachael Saltzman is a lighting director, editor, camera operator, photographer, and fine artist who has worked on such films as *John Wick:* Chapter Two and *The Irishman.*

Charles Salzberg has written nine novels, including five mysteries in his Henry Swann detective series. Books in that series have won a Beverly Hills Book Award and were nominated for two Shamus awards and a David award. Salzberg has also written six nonfiction books. A well-known New York writing teacher, Salzberg also co-founded Greenpoint Press, and was a founding member of the New York Writers Workshop.

Lisa See is a *New York Times* bestselling writer whose first book, *On Gold Mountain*, tells her family's history; she adapted it as an opera libretto for LA Opera. Her critically acclaimed historical novels include *Snow Flower and the Secret Fan*, which was made into a movie. Sees mystery novels include the Edgar-nominated *Flower Net*. She has won a variety of awards, including the Golden Spike Award and the Historymakers Award. See was also named National Woman of the Year by the Organization of Chinese American Women.

Mark Street is a filmmaker who has made both abstract and narrative works. His films have been shown at the Museum of Modern Art in New York, Sundance Film Festival, Tribeca Festival, and other prestigious venues. Street is a professor of visual arts at Fordham University. He is also an essayist and photographer.

Dr. Paula Thomson is professor and director of the Dance program at California State University-Northridge and licensed clinical psychologist in private practice (Los Angeles). She is co-director of the Performance Psychophysiology Laboratory and Professor Emeritus/Senior Scholar at York University (Canada). She is a reliable Adult Attachment Interview coder and conducts research investigating attachment, early trauma, and creativity. She is the co-author of two books, *Creativity and the Performing Artist: Behind the Mask* and *Creativity, Trauma, and Resilience,* and author of multiple chapters and peer-reviewed articles. She was a professional dancer, founded Northern Lights Dance Theatre, and continues to work as a choreographer and movement coach in dance, theater, and opera. Past professional choreographic company work includes Canadian Opera Company, Canadian Stage Company, Stratford Shakespearean Festival, Ballet Jorgen, OperaWorks, and UCLA On the Edge of Chaos. In 2013, she was named one of the top twenty female professors in California.

Jim Tobbe is an acoustic singer-songwriter. He has also written jingles and played in several bands. His album *Reinventing Me* was released in 2020 and is available on Spotify. His son is also a musician and performs as TobyRaps.

Dr. Indre Viskontas is a neuroscientist, musician, opera stage director, and science communicator across all mediums. She is an associate professor of psychology at the University of San Francisco where she runs The Creative Brain Lab and is on faculty at the San Francisco Conservatory of Music. She leads the Communications Core at the Sound Health Network, is the Chair of the Scientific Advisory Board at the NeuroArts Blueprint, and President-Elect of the Society for the Neuroscience of Creativity. She has written more than fifty academic publications on the neural basis of memory, music, and creativity, as well as the book *How Music Can Make You Better.* She has co-hosted several TV and web series, and has appeared on *The Oprah Winfrey Show* and *PBS NewsHour.* She was the host of the popular science podcast *Inquiring Minds,* host and creator of the podcast *Cadence: What music tells us about the mind,* a Webby Awards Honoree, and the host and writer of the Audible Original podcast *Radiant Minds: The World of Oliver Sacks.* She has created four 24-lecture courses for The Great Courses/Wondrium.

Keith Wong is a visual artist, character designer, and animator who has worked on such shows as *Rugrats, Curious George*, and *Trolls.* He has also drawn comic books, illustrated children's books, and created paintings and sculptures.

Preface

This interview is unlike any I've done – wonderful. Just the product itself, that you're making a book about psychology and what's the **heartbeat of the creative person.**

—Doug Jones

We started this journey many years ago, when we realized there was a natural overlap in our interests. Beth, with a background in journalism, had a passion for asking nosy questions and learning people's life stories. She'd always preferred writing feature articles, and her first book, *I'm Too Young to Have Breast Cancer* (Leibson, 2004), shared the personal experiences of sixteen women who were diagnosed with breast cancer before they were forty-five years old.

James, a creativity researcher, was intrigued at the idea of trying a new way of understanding creativity beyond his usual empirical and theoretical work. The first book James ever read about creativity was (appropriately enough) called *Creativity*. It was written by the late Mihaly Csikszentmihalyi (1996) and consisted of interviews with an array of eminent creators. Some were groundbreaking scientists, such as Jonas Salk and Linus Pauling. Others were award-winning writers, such as Nadine Gordimer, Madeline L'Engle, and Naguib Mahfouz. Csikszentmihalyi also spoke with scholars (including Stephen Jay Gould and E. O. Wilson), performers (such as Ed Asner and Oscar Peterson), and others in the public eye (such as Benjamin Spock and Eugene McCarthy). Csikszentmihalyi organized the book around a few core concepts, especially his idea of flow. Also known colloquially as being in the zone, flow is being extremely involved in an activity to the point of losing track of time and one's surroundings. James was instantly hooked on the book – and the field itself. He soon read everything about creativity he could find, and has spent the last quarter-century studying the topic.

Putting Beth's journalistic skill and James's immense knowledge base together, we set out to interview real-life creative people about their lives, inspirations, and influences (well, Beth did the interviews). We began the project without a set mission – we weren't sure who we would interview or what we would find out. The interviews were semi-structured and Beth often followed the lead of the artist, acting more as a journalist than a scholar conducting the type of rigorous qualitative work found in more traditional academic papers. Similarly, we did not start with set categories as in Csikszentmihalyi's (1996) *Creativity*; we spoke to people from a large range of domains, often more curious about interesting stories than big names. When we eventually sorted through all of the interviews, we realized that, although our interviewees encompassed many areas, most were in the arts. One reason may be that, after we had exhausted our friends and acquaintances, Beth tended to approach writers, whereas James was more likely to seek out anyone involved with theater. So, despite James's regular insistence on shaming people who have an arts bias (Kapoor et al., 2024; Patston et al., 2018), we ended up focusing exclusively on artists. Maybe no one will notice?

Once we became aware of our unintended – yet truly personal – focus, we began to reach out to people across a wide spectrum of creative eminence. This decision was partly because of James's emphasis on all levels of creativity, from the personal creativity of mini-c to the everyday creativity of little-c to the experts of Pro-c to those who will be remembered as the creative geniuses of Big-C (Kaufman & Beghetto, 2009, 2023). It was also because the superstars who had agreed to sit down with the legendary Csikszentmihalyi were less inclined to talk to us.

As you will see, we did, eventually, speak to some true superstars with Pulitzer Prizes, Oscars, Grammys, Emmys, *New York Times* bestsellers, and countless other honors and awards to their credit. You'll also meet the people who created *Quantum Leap*, Rambo, Rizzoli and Isles, and *The Gong Show*, alongside people who were key parts of iconic works such as *The Wire, Pan's Labyrinth, Hadestown, Rugrats,* and Woodstock.

Even the people whose creative work you may be less familiar with have eclectic and rich experiences to share. In the pages that follow, you will meet a neuroscientist/opera singer, a co-founder of the leading brand of children's creative activity kits, *Avenue Q*'s original

Christmas Eve, an indie rock singer/bestselling graphic novelist/opera librettist, a stuntman turned television villain, and even a guy who dressed as a green alien and performed his songs in Times Square. Some interviewees have day jobs; others are working artists. Regardless, they all live and breathe creativity.

Our roundabout, somewhat improvised approach ended up making our book quite different from Csikszentmihalyi's (1996) *Creativity*, as well as Susan K. Perry's *Writing in Flow* (1999), which focused exclusively on prominent writers. Most notably, we are not trying to show-case a specific theory, such as flow; we have no set agenda. The stories, memories, and advice you are about to read are as eclectic and varied as the artists themselves.

Acknowledgments

We would like to thank

- Those who helped connect us with the many wonderful creative artists we interviewed for this book: Bill Belmont, Lisa Brody, Gerald Friedler, Gordon Goodman, Donna Mather, Linda McCarter, J. Cleary Rubinos, Meredith Slater, Bruce Smith, Pavitraa Stonecloud, and Elisa Tractman.
- Those who helped us with early versions of our manuscript: Alan Kaufman, Allison Kaufman, Nadeen Kaufman, Weihua Niu, Fatima Rodriguez, Matthew Worwood, and Scott Zachek.
- Stephen Acerra and everyone at Cambridge University Press.

PART I

Childhood

1 | *Supportive Parents*

My parents had more faith in me than I did

What helps a person develop into an artist? Since we're calling this book *The Artist's Life,* it makes sense to start at the very beginning – which would be the parents who raised them. Some people are lucky enough to have parents who are supportive right from the start. Other artists need to win their folks over with hard work, passion, and (at times) a taste of success. There are also those less sterling examples of parenthood, but we will save them for the end of this section. Instead, let's focus first on the moms, dads, siblings, and grandparents who comprised a first appreciative audience.

Let's start with National Book Award-winning novelist **Susan Choi**'s parents, particularly her father. "I think my parents had more faith in me than I did," she told us.

When I was a kid, they were really supportive. They weren't precious about it, but they were very encouraging. I always had the strong sense that they thought my writing was worthwhile and interesting and original. And that it delighted them that I did it. I think it was a little unusual because my father was a Korean immigrant. I'm always meeting other Korean Americans and other Asian Americans of my age who – though it's very stereotypical-sounding – talk about enormous pressure from their immigrant parents to pursue careers that were obviously lucrative and prestigious. I don't know why my father was different. My father put me under enormous pressure to take school seriously and always expected me to get a doctorate in anything, even if I didn't end up being a full-time professor. In that, I've disappointed him. But at the same time, he's a mathematician, and when he saw my early inclination toward literature, he really rolled with it. I enrolled in a doctoral program in English and I dropped out of it. The day I called my father to tell him I was dropping out, I couldn't believe his reaction. He basically said to me, "Good for you. I'm sure you're doing the right thing." Sometimes now I see an academic article on my work by someone who actually did get their doctorate and I'm tickled pink.

We're guessing her dad is, too.

Choi's experience with immigrant parents may not have been a common story, but it was one she shared with writer **Gina B. Nahai:**

My parents were very supportive. It's strange, because I was sure my parents, who paid for my education, would be very disappointed that I didn't finish law school. But my parents were always untraditional. The reason they left Iran when they did, and sent my sister and me to boarding school, was that they always wanted their daughters to have careers and a real education. My dad said, "You know, it's better to be a good writer than a mediocre lawyer. If you don't want to be a lawyer, it's better to do what you really feel like doing."

Parents Who Were Wary of the Arts

Actor-writer **Jim Piddock**'s father was encouraging, despite his own less-than-positive associations with entertainers. "My father had a very normal job," he told us.

He worked for ICI as a technical adviser. He was like a doctor for crops, going around Kent and consulting with farmers. His father, my grandfather, was a pretty irresponsible guy; he left my dad and his two siblings for a chorus girl. My grandmother couldn't raise three boys on her own, so she gave the middle one away and that was my father. He was raised by an aunt who had a bit of money, so he went to a better school and all that, but I think he probably had a lifelong feeling of abandonment. It was only in my late teens that I discovered my family background in show business when my dad said, "That's my half sister on television there."

It turned out that his father, Harry Piddock, was an actor and a comedian, who had a music hall act with Charlie Chaplin before Chaplin left for America. Fortunately, my father was still supportive of me becoming an actor, even though the effects of that profession had affected his life very negatively as a child. I ended up looking up some of his extended family and finding them. I lived around the corner from one of them and they became some of my closest relatives.

Like Piddock, singer **Country Joe McDonald** had a father who had a hard relationship with the arts. In McDonald's case, it was his father's own thwarted ambitions:

My father grew up on a farm in the Depression era and at one point got a guitar and brought it home. His father was a minister and made him take it back. My father always struggled with trying to play a musical instrument. He was essentially a creative person. His approach to farming was very creative, his approach to life was creative. You know, people who do labor can be very creative – mechanics and farmers. They can be very creative in the way they approach their work. But my father could never do music. Whatever it was inside of him got damaged, and it was a frustration for his whole life. We used to buy him simpler and simpler instruments to play and he never could play any instrument, although he liked music and he was proud of me. He wrote a book, his autobiography, a very wonderful book. And he could bake bread and do leather tooling and he used to work with horses. But again, he got stifled, and I was allowed to blossom. My mother gave me music lessons and nobody ever told me, "This is crap, don't do it."

Parents Who Were Fully Supportive

Musician **Bruce Mack**'s mother and brother were both helpful influences:

My mother, who loved music, turned me on to a lot of Etta James and King Pleasure. Listening to those records really got my interest. I started reading about the artists who created those records and the producers behind them. That stirred me up. Between that and listening to radio, I was drawn into music. My brother, who could sing very well, babysat me. He also had a trumpet I didn't hear much, but I loved the glow of it. He would sing television commercials with me. As I got older, and started to express a certain interest in music, my mother gave me an allowance so that I could go and buy the latest 45 vinyl disc. She didn't tell me what to get, she just said, "Here's the money for it, pick your song." We had a small turntable, but she eventually purchased a stereo for the house that I was the manager of. I learned every button on it, learned about the needle, even how to tweak the contour on my own.

Musician **Peter Litvin**'s parents were also supportive:

As a kid, my thing was guitar and recording. I didn't have money for equipment, so I would get recording gear for my birthday and Christmas presents. When I didn't have anyone to play music with me, my mom got a drum set and started taking drum lessons. She wanted to jam with me. As the years went by, they observed that I wanted to make a career out of it and was capable of doing it professionally. My parents never once told me, "Don't follow your dreams," or "Go get a real job." They always supported my music and creativity.

Phyllis Brody, a visual artist and entrepreneur who founded a successful company producing arts activities, received maternal support through the gift of time. "My mother was a very special and encouraging person," Brody said.

She loved to experiment with cooking, sewing, and making things, and she understood that I had this passion, too. She never asked me to do chores because she wanted to support my being busy doing all these other creative things and that was more important than me learning how to do the dishes and dust. I'm sure that had a lot to do with the fact that creativity became so important to me.

"We always had music in our lives," singer-songwriter **Julie Gold** told us.

There was a swing set in the backyard and I would swing and sing to the birdies and the cat. I started out playing for animals on a little plastic toy keyboard. Then my parents bought a little piano and I was always at the piano. The minute my parents thought I was good, they gave me a better piano. My parents were unconditionally supportive of the arts for both me and my brother. It was part our life like anything else – it held equal if not more importance.

Non-fiction writer **Mary Roach**'s father appreciated her art more than she thought was warranted:

I never played a musical instrument as a kid, but I drew – not in any kind of impressive way. But as a little kid, I was always drawing little books. I'd staple them together. My father was artistically very gifted so he would take my horrible fingerpainting smears and frame them and put them up. I have memories of some of the pieces of quote-unquote "art" because they were on the wall in our home. Some of them look like Franz Kline, pretty abstract. I didn't write; it wasn't something I wanted to do. I mean, I wrote because I had to, but I wasn't a kid who wrote stories other than for school. All in all, I don't think I was terribly creative as a kid.

Roach's father's encouragement may not have led her to become a visual artist, but she has seen tremendous success as a *New York Times* bestselling author.

Artist and animator **Keith Wong** lucked out; both his parents were active, hands-on champions of his early efforts:

My parents were both teachers, but my dad was pretty much an artist. He would draw me and my brother. He would build us dioramas and machines and airplanes; he would create just things for us. He would go to the junkyard and take a barrel and cut the center out and put in car seats and steering wheels and switches and dials so it looked like you were in a cockpit. He found these industrial springs that he would weld on so it would be on this little rocking thing, but it was very much like a little jet fighter with all these little switches ... My mom would make us costumes and whatnot for Halloween. They wanted to show us music and places, concerts in the park, or they would just take us to see color and shapes and museums, even when we were almost too young to absorb it. But we did. My parents were very supportive of our creative endeavors and continue to be to this day.

Photographer/lighting programmer **Rachael Saltzman**'s mother took a situation that might have angered other parents and turned it into a lifelong opportunity for growth:

Around first grade, I'd decided that I didn't need to go to school anymore. It was dull, I was at the top of my class and bored out of my mind. In the middle of class, I told my teacher as much, and headed for the door. She asked where I was going, and I told her, "home." And I did. I think teachers of six-year-olds don't usually have to deal with that sort of thing, so she wasn't sure how to stop me. I walked home, got there around lunchtime, and told my mom what had happened. Over lunch, my mom explained to me that I couldn't do that – or, rather, shouldn't, as I clearly had just done so. We made a deal. Within reason, if I didn't feel like I could handle school that day, she'd call in for me. On those days, we went to historical sites, museums, shows, the library. I learned more outside of school, thanks to an involved parent, than I ever did sitting through class.

Parental Inspiration

There is parental support, and then there are parents who serve as a role model. Musician **Jacob Hyman** was inspired by his father's work. "My dad's a musician," he told us.

He has this crazy technical knowledge and innate ability. He's got almost perfect pitch. He can play anything by ear on the piano; he also plays the accordion, the clarinet, the drums, and the guitar. My parents tried to get me to play piano. I took lessons on three separate occasions from different teachers. I was just never really motivated. I think it was partially the piano. Some things come naturally to me, but piano is certainly not one of them. Reading music is also not one of them. That was really frustrating to me, trying to get this technical knowledge of something that my brain seemed to not want. I'm very math resistant. After I stopped with the piano, I took my first drum lesson in school with the band. My parents got me a used drum set for my birthday and that was it.

Lisa Brody also had a mother who was an artist and passed along her passion. "Every day we did something creative in terms of art, whether it was drawing in a coloring book or more massive creative projects around the house. I would spend hours in my room doing art. I didn't want my artwork hung, I didn't want to show it to anyone, I just did it for myself."

But not everyone gets their talent from their parents. **Cecil Castellucci**'s multifaceted talents span writing, music, and film, whereas their parents were scientists. Despite the differences, their parents were able to nurture Castelluci's creative passions:

My parents do research; they're trying to figure out stories. They're trying to figure out genetics, but it's really about the story. For me, I don't see any difference; it's the same thing. My mother likes to tell the story of when I was like three years old, and she came into the living room and I was sobbing. My mom asked, "What is going on, what's wrong?" I said, "It's the saddest thing I've ever seen." PBS was on, and it was a show about Trojan women in ancient Greece with subtitles. But I couldn't read, so my mom asked, "How do you know what's going on?" I told her it was because I could see how the people were interacting; I knew what was happening. I think that was the moment where my mom realized, this girl is not going to be a scientist – she's going to be an artist. I think because she recognized that, she encouraged any sort of creative things that I wanted to do. For example, when I was really little, my mom had this book that she used to try to get my brother and me to play all the time called *Let's Play Math*. I didn't like that boring game. But if it had been *Let's Tell a Story* or *Let's Make Something Up*, then I would have played it.

"When I was four years old," Castellucci said, "my mom started taking me to the opera, the ballet, and to New York City to see fancy movies."

My favorite opera was *The Magic Flute*. Whenever we traveled anywhere, to visit a house or something like that, I was always interested in the story. What's the story here? What's the story of the house? How did the people feel when they lived here? What were they like? What was the difference between the people who were upstairs and downstairs? Who would I have been in this place? We always did stuff and talked about stories. Even to this day, one of us will read a book and then we'll get everybody else to read it, and then whenever we're all in the same city, we'll have a conversation about it.

Parents can be a driving force in a young artist's life, as we have seen (and will continue to see). From modeling creative values and behavior to offering opportunities and resources to ensuring a child grows up loved, great parents are an inspiration that can continue to have an effect into adulthood. Artist **Isabelle Bryer** told us:

I used art to make myself feel better about being homesick and so far away from my family in France. When I painted something, I took a photo and mailed it to my mother. She ended up having mounds of photos of every painting I had ever made – the ugly ones, the good ones, the tiny ones. She kept them all.

2 | *The Extended Family*
We all ended up in the arts

What's better than having supportive parents? How about having an entire family cheering you on? Three-time Jewish National Book Award-winning writer **Dara Horn** was encouraged not only by her mother and father but also by her three siblings. "I come from a very creative family," she told us. "I have two sisters and a brother and all of us are in creative fields." Indeed, all four Horns have reached artistic success – brother Zach is an Emmy-winning art director and editor, sister Ariel Horn Levenson is a novelist and teacher, and sister Jordana Horn is a journalist and lawyer.

People ask me if my parents are artists or writers. And the short answer is no. My father is a dentist and my mother is a public school teacher with a doctorate. But my parents raised us in a very creative way. My mother is very good at focusing people's talents. She saw early on that my brother had artistic talent. She started steering him toward art and asked the art teacher at the public school to give him lessons. My mother never pressured us in any way. She would see what we wanted to do and she would find creative ways to encourage us.

I was writing all the time. When I was six years old, my mom gave me a diary. I didn't really know what a diary was, so I wrote it like a book. Like, "One day I went to school and such and such happened. The next day ..." At some point, I must have read something about a diary and learned it's supposed to read "Dear Diary" and have the date at the top. So suddenly there's a change and it was "Dear Diary," because I was copying that model. I also had a separate book of stories that I made up. One was about a dinosaur egg and what if it hatched? Another was a story from the perspective of a baby in its mother's stomach and it's walking around and exploring different parts of the body – "Oh, I wonder what's in the nose?" They weren't long, like two pages.

We traveled a lot when I was growing up, not for my family's work. They took us on trips to places where most people would not think to take four kids, like Cambodia and Peru. (But is it a vacation if you have to get a shot?) They realized that they had to develop a strategy for making sure we didn't bother the flight attendants on the long flights, so they told us we had to keep a journal. I took it very seriously. I kept detailed journals, and that was how I developed as a writer. The first time I ever published anything was when I was fourteen years old. It was an essay adapted from a travel journal that I kept. My sisters also kept journals, and my brother kept sketchbooks on these trips. That was probably only once a year. We couldn't go to Cambodia every day.

Horn's essay was published in *Hadassah* magazine – and was nominated for a National Magazine Award.

Horn's mother had many ideas of how to inspire creativity in her children.

My mother would have us do group projects. We would come home and she'd say, "Why don't you guys write a play and we'll perform it after dinner?" And we would. That happened all the time. This is still a family tradition we do even now as adults. We write poems and songs for our parents on their birthdays and anniversaries. It's funny, because now that I have children, I realize that part of it was just a coping strategy to get us out of her hair. But it was also something she did very consciously, because she was a teacher.

Being in a family with four kids who are very close in age, there was a lot of competition for attention. Whenever we sat down for dinner, it was impossible for anybody to get a word in because we were all talkative and always competing for my parents' attention. And it drove them crazy. One day my mother came home from work with a kitchen timer. She put it on the table at dinner time and said, "From now on, each child will have five minutes to tell about their day. And anyone who interrupts that child will have time deducted." One result from this is that I speak very quickly. But another result of this is that my siblings couldn't put up with the idea that they couldn't offer their running commentary about what happened during your day. One of my sisters passed out cards at the table and we would write down numbers and hold them up while one of us was speaking. Rating the day: Your day gets 2.3, your day gets -5, like at the Olympics. I think when you're speaking in front of an audience and they're holding up numbers saying that your day stinks, it makes you very aware of how to tell a story and keep an audience engaged.

The prize-winning novelist has certainly put that skill to good use.

Novelist and journalist **Dana Sachs** also has creative siblings; both her brother Ira and her sister Lynne are successful filmmakers. "I have a theory that we all ended up in the arts," she told us,

because my dad was such a creative person and my mom was so interested in learning and reading and studying. My dad is much more unconventional than her. For example, he would drive around and pull the Christmas trees out that people had left by their trash cans. He'd get dozens of them and stick them in his front yard. It was just a weird thing that he did. My mom is much more conservative as a person than him, but we learned about the value of education from her. The combination of education and openness and possibility that we got from our parents led to us wanting to live creative lives.

Sometimes, a sibling can be the ultimate partner in crime (or should we say creativity?). Playwright **John Patrick Bray** shared with us:

I'm an identical twin and, growing up, my brother and I were always inventing games with one another and telling each other stories. My mother told us that we had created our own language before we learned English. It was a gibberish language, unique to us, that we used to communicate, and mostly to make each other laugh. We both had asthma, so we had to spend a lot of time indoors, especially during the winter. We spent a lot of time playing with action figures; we'd give them our own names and set up stories for them, rather than following whatever world of story they came from – G.I. Joe, Universal Monsters, Indiana Jones, Star Wars, Zorro, etc. So, we both became storytellers early on. Through our movies, my brother and I continue telling stories and playing.

Indeed, two of the films Bray has written were directed by his brother Gregg Bray.

Actress **Donna Lynne Champlin** and her brother, filmmaker/archivist Mike Champlin, could make a game out of anything. "I lucked out brother-wise because he is also extremely creative," she said.

Our mother always encouraged us to use our imaginations. I remember my brother and I many times created a restaurant downstairs and invited my mom to dinner and a show. She'd sit there and pretend to munch on paper food and applaud our musical numbers until we were finished. We used to make audio tapes with our attempts at old-timey radio shows. We made up a game where we'd sit at opposite ends of the kitchen table, drink different-colored sodas and try to make the other person laugh so the soda would come out of their nose and fly out towards the center of the plastic tablecloth. Clearly, the person who could make the other person laugh harder, making their soda go further toward the center of the table, won. Just doing spit takes didn't count – the soda had to come out your nose.

Sometimes, family friends can be the ones who help nurture young artists. "My parents surrounded themselves with creative people," visual artist/musician **Tine Kindermann** told us.

They decided they didn't want to have a television; also, they were very poor so they certainly couldn't have afforded a TV at the time. My parents had friends who were artists who would come by and would draw with my brother and me. That was something I was always really looking forward to. We took a workshop on marionette-making from a real marionette-maker. When I was about four years old, I had a corner in the room that I shared with my brother that I'd separated from the rest of the room with a little bookshelf. I had a little table in there and it was my graphic design office. We were creative in so many ways. We would dress up our stuffed animals and play these adventures with them. I remember one time we had learned about the Vikings and how the Vikings had discovered America, so we dressed up all our stuffed animals and made them green felt costumes and they were all going across the ocean to end up in America. We had this one old teddy bear that had an eye missing and you could take off the head. We decided that he was the dead grandfather who would be returned to the land of his forefathers and we put him in a shoebox. Then we went to my mother who was making honey cake, and asked if we could have some for the bear. Because we knew about burial rites, we knew the bear needed something to eat on his journey to the Other World.

Supportive Grandparents

When parents do not encourage their child's creative efforts, a loving grandparent can step up to fill the void. Lyricist **Michael Colby** remembers that

my grandparents were a bigger influence on my life than my parents. My maternal grandparents owned the Algonquin Hotel, which played a large part in the theatrical community. I was surrounded by theater; my first show was when I was six years old. I grew up privileged to see the golden age of the American musical theater. There was this paradox: I was an outsider at school, yet elsewhere I led a kind of Jewish prince life. I got to hobnob with people in the theater. Oscar Peterson played at my bar mitzvah; I had breakfast with Ella Fitzgerald. I was taken to opening nights by playwrights who were impressed by my knowledge of theater history at a young age. It was a charmed life. When my little brother and I spent time in Beverly Hills with my grandparents, we were constantly mistaken for Liz Taylor's children, who were in the bungalow next to us. It was a fantastic life ... But my parents had harrowing personal problems, always fighting. Protectively, I never used drugs or alcohol or anything like that – I had enough neurosis at home. I didn't want to lose control like I witnessed on a daily basis. Maybe that's why I was creative from an early age: It was an outlet for seeing a better, happier world. Or at least a world where you could sing and dance and not hear a lot of *Sturm und Drang* going on daily. However, my grandparents were always very supportive about my working in the theater. They were my safe harbor.

Writer **Charles Salzberg** found a role model and source of nurturance in his grandmother:

She was a wonderful storyteller. When we went on car trips, I would sit in the back seat with my grandmother and she would tell me the stories of movies she had seen. It was actually better than being at the movies. She always wanted to be a writer. She stopped school when she was twelve, was married when she was fifteen years old. She had my mother before she was sixteen. But she was always reading. My father never read a book in his life. He didn't understand me and he didn't understand what I wanted to do. When I was getting ready to go to college, he said, "Just take accounting courses." I was pretty strong-willed. My mother wasn't an interfering mother so she didn't say anything, but she wasn't particularly supportive. When I started a career as a freelance writer, she used to give me want ads for jobs – "real jobs," she would say. She didn't understand the creative life either. The only one who did was my grandmother.

Just about everyone we spoke with had someone in their corner, whether a family member, friend, or teacher, who encouraged their creativity – or at least understood the impulse to create.

3 | *Parents Who Came Around*
Once they saw I was serious

Not everyone receives unconditional encouragement in childhood. Sometimes, parents are simply indifferent. They might be neither positive nor negative influences, such as those of musician-theater artist **Steve Riffkin**. "Teachers appreciated what I did," he told us.

But my parents were always very low-key about handing out praise. I'll never fully understand what that was all about, why they seemed to be so careful about that. Maybe it was for a good reason – maybe they didn't want me to get a big head. But they were not doting parents; they were not the kind of parents that glommed onto any little artistic thing I did. They just weren't that type. My parents never did the whole, "Get up and play for Aunt Sadie" thing.

Actor-writer-record producer **Bruce Kimmel**'s parents were similarly uninterested.

I had a very strange family and they didn't really care about kids at all. I don't know if that's fair to say, but I don't think they ever really wanted kids. You had children back then because that's what you were supposed to do. They didn't encourage me. In fact, they were negative about certain aspects of what I did as a performer. They would say, "Oh, you can't sing. Don't sing." Unpleasant. That's not a good thing to say to a child – although I didn't listen, thankfully. My mother's favorite expression was: "Go play in traffic." It's not like today where you can't say those things to kids. A good day for them was when we would leave at nine in the morning and come back at five. Unlike today, we didn't have cell phones; they didn't check up on us. They just said, "You're going to play? Good, great, see you later." It was a very different time back then and, in some ways, a much better time for kids because I could just go out on my own and discover. If you scraped your knee, you scraped your knee. You lived. To me, today is so overprotective, it's not fun anymore.

Musician **Jim Tobbe** has reflected on his lack of parental support – and has changed the cycle for his own children.

I worked professionally as a jingle writer. When I was in college, when we were sponsored by Miller Beer, I got to do the tour bus thing and play in front of bands like the Atlanta Rhythm Section and Pure Prairie League. I got a little taste of the life of a musician. But I always wonder, if I had that support from my parents and from the people around me, how would that have changed my life? I believe it would have changed mine significantly. I think artists who never really make it – and, in particular, musicians – end up wondering about that. But I also think that not having the support charged me up. I wanted to prove that I could do it because I knew that I had the ability to do it, and I still know I have the ability to do it. Now I'm at peace with that, I don't need to be in a band right now. I have told my kids that whatever they decide they want to do with their life, as long as they show me that they really want to do it, I will support them in any way I can. I don't ever want to be a stumbling block for either one of my kids.

And his approach has paid off. Tobbe's son is also a musician; he performs as TobyRaps.

Sometimes, artists learn deeper lessons when they reflect on why their parents were unsupportive. Writer **Peggy Orenstein** remembered,

I went through a phase in high school where I got interested in gothic and horror. I read a lot of Shirley Jackson and tried to imitate her style in short stories for my school literary magazine. My parents became alarmed and told me I couldn't publish those stories or even show them to anyone because they were deranged and disturbed. I was very resentful, but I turned in the stories anyway and one of them made it into print. Looking back, I realize my attempts at horror were pretty unskilled. I see why they were upset, but I'm impressed by my defiance. It was ultimately a good lesson, both in terms of following your gut – I have had to shut out a lot of doubting voices over the years – and for me as a parent. That impulse to censor your child's work when it threatens you is not about protecting *them*, it's about your fear of how *you'll* be judged.

Changing Their Tune

Many parents who are initially hesitant can be won over and even turn into their kid's biggest cheerleaders. Muralist **David Guinn**'s father was encouraging, albeit with concerns:

My father would give me positive feedback about what I was doing. At the same time, he clearly said, "Don't be an artist. Do something else." He felt like art was what he *had* to do; he didn't think he could do something else.

But when I was in college, he said, "If you can do something else, then do it because being an artist is a really hard life." So there were mixed messages . . . I do think it's a hard life, but it's something that I'm still working at. I don't think that I could *not* do it.

Many parents, whether artists themselves, artistically inclined, or working in an unrelated area, focused on the question of earning a living. Actor **Michael Kostroff** remembered that

when I was little, before there was a threat of me becoming a professional, my parents were somewhat supportive. They were both artistic. They played instruments, they took us to the theater, they took us to concerts. And they both worked in film and television, on the production side, not as performers. I grew up in New York City, which was a great place for the arts. So there is a little bit of the nature/nurture question. They exposed me to a lot of artistic things, so it wasn't foreign or weird to them. They appreciated things like music and theater and the arts. But they were also well aware of how difficult it was financially – only the slimmest margin of actors make a living, the very lucky ones. They were discouraging in that they wanted me to have something to fall back on. I think they were nervous about that part of it.

Fashion designer **Doub Hanshaw**'s parents were happy with her foray into art until it became a career possibility. "My parents were open to me being creative," she said.

My mother was a painter. My parents were supportive of my interest in art history; when I was a teenager, my mother was very upset that I didn't know who Robert Mapplethorpe was. However, they were not excited about me becoming an artist. They were concerned about how I would make a living. They were surprised when I went into fashion.

Hobby vs. Career

Actor **Maurice Godin**'s parents saw the arts as a hobby at best, not a career. "My dad was an iron worker," he told us.

My mom was a stay-at-home mom until she got a job in retail, later in life. Neither of my parents had much experience with creativity, but if my dad had had other options when he was younger, he might have gone into music or singing because he really enjoyed it. I remember going on vacation with the family when I was younger and there would always be a couple of relatives with guitars in the kitchen of my grandparents' farmhouse. There was a lot of smoking and drinking and they'd all be singing songs, but they never thought of music as a career; that was just part of home life on weekends. My parents never encouraged the arts as a serious endeavor; it was a time-waster for them. It was a big pill to swallow for my folks when I told them I wanted to go into theater. My dad was desperate for me to become an engineer or something. They were really worried about it. My mother tolerated my desire to become an actor and my dad hoped I would get over it. Even though I went to university and four years of conservatory training in acting, I think he was always hoping that I would either do commercials – because that would be the only way to make a living at it – or that I would use my drawing skills to be an engineer. His big solution to the whole thing: "You know, you can be a theater engineer." That was his compromise.

Visual artist **Lex Marie**'s mother was supportive of her passion for art, so long as she had a college degree to fall back on. "I was raised by my mother," she said.

She took notice of my interest in art, so she would always find me paint sets and markers. In the 1990s, there were so many infomercials for art kits, and she would give me some of those. I think a lot of parents say, "You can't do art. You're not going to make money, so it can just be a hobby." I wanted to go to an art institute or art school, but my mother said, "You have to go to college. I don't care what you major in; you just have to go." I ended up going to a university by my home. But my mother accepted I would study art, and she encouraged it. I'm thankful for that, because I truly did not enjoy any other subject. She didn't go to college herself; my sisters and I were first-generation Americans and first-generation college graduates. From that position, her mindset was that college was the one way to have security in life and finances.

Eventually, Marie's mother saw her faith in her daughter pay off. "My mother walked into my first solo show," Marie told us, "and she started crying. It was the first time she really understood what I was trying to do. She said, 'Oh, I finally get it now.' She also saw I was able to support myself and my son."

Writer **Tess Gerritsen**'s parents' responses were a mixed bag. "When I told my father that I wanted to become a writer," she said, "he was really quite dubious. It has to do with the Asian American conservatism when it comes to careers. He felt, rightly so, that very few people make money at writing so he directed me toward medicine." In fact, Gerritsen was a successful physician before becoming a novelist.

My parents were supportive of writing as a hobby, but they weren't supportive of me trying to make that my career. My mom had a slightly different attitude than my dad because she was a direct immigrant from China and she came from a very well-to-do family that was quite cultured. Her grandfather was a well-known poet in China, so she did have a literary background there. In her mind, a writing career was fine. But she could hardly speak English. I remember vividly, I think I might have been five years old, and I asked my mother how to spell "grape" and she proceeded to very confidently tell me it was "grap." I learned quickly that I couldn't trust her spelling.

Indre Viskontas, like Gerritsen, blends the arts and sciences. She has a PhD in neuroscience and is a successful professor and researcher – as well as a professional opera singer.

My parents were supportive of us finding things that we liked to do. Whatever we got into, whether it was piano or dance or the clarinet, we had to do it a lot. It wasn't like you could just explore; you had to take lessons and you had to practice. They instilled the drive to work very hard. But they also, being immigrants, had a very pragmatic mentality. The idea of making a life as an artist was not acceptable. It was too difficult. You had to get a good job and a good, solid education. You could do all that other stuff on the side, but your main focus should be on academic subjects or getting some kind of degree that will guarantee you a place in society of some respect and economic stability. We were all workhorses. My brother is an orthopedic surgeon and all my cousins have medical or engineering degrees. That drive to make sure that you had a good solid education to fall back on, in contrast to the celebration of life in all these other avenues, led me to where I am today – which is straddling both science and art in a precarious balance.

Other artists had parents who were reluctant at first but were won over by hard work – and success. Novelist **Diana Abu-Jaber** told us,

My father and his side of the family were serious storytellers. I grew up listening to their stories. My father used his food as the springboard for telling us stories about his past. He was truthfully very creative, but he didn't recognize it. I liked to write down my stories; that was my chance to get my own words in because my father and uncles were so much louder than I was. My father felt that an acceptable career meant being a lawyer, doctor, or engineer. Being a writer was synonymous with being a ne'er-do-well. The writers were like the jugglers and the clowns; the goofballs, the homeless people by the side of the road back in the old country. You would never wish that on your children. He was not encouraging when I majored in English literature. It used to be very distressing for him. He asked me over and over again, "What is your major?" He kept hoping that my answer would change. But then, I published my first novel and started giving readings and he saw people in the audience. He heard people asking me questions about my work and taking it seriously. Then it all started to turn around for him, but he needed that additional component before he could really accept it.

Novelist **Chang-rae Lee** had a similar experience:

My mother liked to draw. She wasn't an artist, but she had an artistic sensibility. So, she didn't mind my creativity. I wrote poetry and stories. I loved books and read everything I could get my hands on – I took out books at whatever limit they had at the public library. But I didn't really think I could be a writer. It was not feasible in any realm I could imagine. I didn't think it was part of my future. My immigrant parents certainly didn't want me to get into a line of work that was so unstable financially. So naturally they weren't initially thrilled, but once they saw I was serious about making a go at it, they became very supportive, both financially and emotionally. To be honest, I couldn't have even attempted writing if I hadn't had their blessing, because I would have felt so guilty for going against their wishes. They didn't emigrate to this country so that I could be destitute and obscure, a poor artist or writer. They came for financial security and a different life from what they might have expected in the old country. But after the education that I received, and all the other intellectual and artistic training that I'd gotten over the years, I guess they recognized that this was something I could at least attempt.

Sometimes parents can come around even if they started out being actively discouraging. Dancer **Samantha Jakus** remembered,

I wanted to do tumbling so bad and my mom wouldn't sign me up for it. Maybe it was financial. She had four kids, my dad was sick, and she was going to have to take time to bring me. She didn't know she was purposely not giving me what I needed. Right before high school, I started paying for my own classes and I did that for seven years. My mom was worried about me going in for dance, always asking the same question: "How are you going to pay for this?" She didn't come to many of my shows. It's weird, she's so supportive now. She brought a whole bus to come to the STREB show.

The STREB Extreme Action Company, which Jakus performed with for many years, describes itself as an extreme-action dance troupe.

Success Speaks Louder than Words

Actor **Doug Jones**'s father was cautious until he experienced his son's talent in person. "I came from a very cynical Midwestern family," he told us.

My dad was a self-starter entrepreneur who had his own consulting firm. My dad had a very good business sense, he had a PhD in education and taught college classes on the side, and he also ran for public office in the Indiana State Legislature. He was an I-can-do-anything sort of person; he searched out opportunities and created his own. He also understood the artistic brain. On the weekends, my dad would take the family to movies and he loved, loved, loved musicals – Gene Kelly and Fred Astaire. I grew up watching them on TV with my dad, and him saying, "You've got to see this." He loved that, so he understood my artistic side that wanted to be in those things. Watching my very stressed-out dad smile and laugh and enjoy some-thing on the weekends, understanding what that weekend uplifting escape could do for people – I wanted to be a part of what *that* was.

Now, my mom and my dad and my three older brothers all have a good sense of humor. It's a big laugh riot with us whenever we get together. So when one of the fold says, "I want to be a performer, I want to be on TV," you get a lot of eye rolling, a lot of "yeah, yeah, try again" – you know, the things that families do to each other. And when you're living in Indiana, show biz doesn't seem like a viable career choice. At first, as any sensible parent or sibling would do, I'd get a tap on the head – "that's cute, but what do you really want to do?" And when it came to choosing a major for college, if my parents were going to help me pay for school, I was not allowed to major in theater even though I wanted to. So I majored in radio and television broadcasting, because it had more of a business bent to it that could translate into other types of jobs. But I minored in theater. That was the compromise. Again, my family was realistic. They all had talents and goals of their own, and I was this artistic "oh, I want to be on stage dancing and singing and performing" guy. They thought it was adorable, but it didn't make sense to them. Any responsible family in the Midwest would have this attitude because of the basic odds of being successful in any of the arts. A responsible parent looking at those odds should encourage his kid to make his way in the world in a way that's not that. It was really more not wanting to encourage me to go into the life of a bohemian artist who might be starving most of my life.

In my freshman year at Ball State University, I was part of a folk-dance troupe; we did dances from all over the world. We had a big spring show and my parents drove from Minneapolis to come see the show. When the show was finished, I saw my parents in about the fifth row, dead center, and my dad standing and applauding at the end of the show with a two-foot pearly white smile. It was a rare sight for me because of how driven and stressed out he was during the week. He'd just had his weekend escape, one of those escapes I loved watching and being a part of when I was a kid. But now I was on stage being a part of it. I went home for the weekend right after that show and my dad and I were sitting in the kitchen, alone, which in a huge family is a rare moment. He asked me, "Are you going to be a part of that dance troupe again next year?" I said, "Gosh, I don't know. As with any artistic bunch of people thrown into a room together, there was a lot of drama, a lot of personalities constantly trying to stir up things. I don't like negative drama, I really don't. Some of the dancers were divas, and I don't want to be a part of the politics and drama. It's a bit too much for me to want to go back there again. I might just finish this up and then go onto something else next year." My dad said, "Oh, I think that's a mistake. I think that's probably one of the best things you've ever been a part of." For him to tell me to spend my time on that creative thing meant the world to me. That talk with him was one of our last times together. He passed away a month later, just as I was about to come home for the summer.

As we have seen, some parents and families serve as inspirations whose devotion to and belief in their children's artistic potential are grounded in their love. Others are indifferent (or worse), or else worried about the harsh realities of the artistic life, wanting more security and stability for their children – but once they have seen evidence of a child's persistence and talent, they, too, may end up being a groundswell of support. An astute reader may have noticed that we have no horror stories of truly terrible parents. You shouldn't assume that we didn't hear any such stories. Rather, in every case, we were ultimately asked to not include them in this book. It is safe to say, however, that many artists had difficult upbringings; indeed, research shows that genius-level creators are a bit more likely to have troubled childhoods (Simonton, 2009). We are, of course, not suggesting that families should jumpstart their kids' careers by creating obstacles. We've already heard from plenty of well-supported artists who blossomed into successes.

Families are but one childhood influence (for better or worse) on young artists. There's also a life outside the home. Children spend more than 15,000 hours in school (Sanchez, 2023), and their experiences there can make a big impact. In the last two chapters in this section, we will talk about how artists remember their early educational experiences.

4 | *School through an Artist's Eyes*
You passed because you're just going to be an artist

Many artists saw school as something akin to a speedbump – a moderate annoyance, but one to simply be navigated. For example, writer **Dara Horn** told us, "I was a nerdy good student, so whatever they told me to do, I would do. School wasn't very important in developing my writing."

What was relevant for her, however, was entering a gifted program, at the Center for Talented Youth at Johns Hopkins University, when she was twelve years old.

It was supposed to be for people who had the ability to take the SAT as middle school students. I took a writing course for three summers. It was very intense; it's like you did a semester in six weeks because you were in class from 9 a.m. to 3 p.m., and then you did your assignments in the evening. I remember it very vividly because that was the first time anybody ever taught me how to write. They would teach that in a way that was clear for twelve-year-olds. They would have us do exercises like, "Write about the experience of walking through some thick snow without using any adverbs." It forced you to write in a different way. Another one was, "Describe this fork without using your sense of sight," or, "Write about a dinner using only your sense of smell." This was all nonfiction writing, so the purpose was to produce essays. I remember the teacher would say, "I know you learned the 1, 2, 3 method, which is that each essay should be five paragraphs long. The first paragraph is the introduction, and the last sentence of that paragraph tells you what the main idea is. Then there are three more paragraphs that are supporting three pieces of evidence, and then your last paragraph is a rewriting of your introduction, repeating what you said before. We're never doing this again. This is not what an essay is. You're allowed to do this when you're writing an exam. If you're not writing an exam, you're never allowed to write this way ever again." And we read then-contemporary writers I had never heard of in school – Joan Didion, Annie Dillard, Phillip Lopate. That was hugely important to me. Then I took a fiction course there, which made me feel like I would never be able to write fiction; I thought that I would never be able to make up a story.

Horn would not pursue fiction until she had graduated from high school:

I started being published as a teenager, and in high school and college I was writing as a journalist. All my summer jobs in college were at magazines. I worked at *The New Republic*, *Time*, *Newsweek*, and *American Heritage*, and I thought that was the way to be paid for writing. I remember doing an interview for a fellowship after college and they asked me, "You're such a good writer, why don't you ever try to write fiction?" I said, 'I don't think I can make anything up." But I got that fellowship, and that was the year I wrote my first novel.

Singer-songwriter **Julie Gold** also received her real education outside of the traditional classroom, but her circumstances were quite different. "Freshman year in college," she said,

I was underage but I got a job in a bar. It was owned by a very eccentric woman who carried a pistol. The building was known to be haunted. There was a tarot card reader upstairs, and it had a mystical feel. I would unplug the Pong machine, turn off the jukebox, and then sit at the piano. Everyone smoked and everyone drank. I would play the Beatles, Motown, Carole King, and then throw in a song of mine. The audience consisted of everyone – college students and Vietnam vets and Mafia guys. All sorts of persuasions. The noise didn't bother me; the smoke didn't bother me. If I had a final the next day, somehow I did it. That was my education, when I was at college. I was already writing my songs. I didn't have any composition; I didn't have any of the skills. I love music and I make music, but I can't write music and I have no theory. The professors do theory. It's like saying, "I love Italian food, so I'm an Italian scholar." I wasn't accepted to Temple's School of Music.

But that doesn't seem to have been an impenetrable roadblock for Gold.

Visual artist **Isabelle Bryer** was able to find a place to pursue art in school – eventually. "Growing up in France," she said, "I didn't particularly enjoy school. I would have rather stayed home with my brothers. It became more interesting when I started art classes. That is when I realized I wanted to go in this direction."

Arts vs. Academics

When students' artistic pursuits were better known at school, they may have had a very different educational experience. For muralist **David**

Guinn, artwork allowed him another way to complete assignments. "In middle school and high school," he said,

there'd be options to write a paper or do an art project. For instance, in senior year, we did an American history thesis, but I was able to make a model of something rather than write a paper on it. I chose that route over and over again of making things and using that aesthetic or visual talent or skill. At one point when I was taking the PSAT, I had to write down what I thought I was going to do, and I put down engineering. I look back now and wonder what that path would have been like.

Artist and animator **Keith Wong** had a similar experience. "I was so obsessed with art and music and whatever I could do creatively, that I wasn't that good in any of the other academic subjects," he told us.

When I was in seventh grade, two of my friends were taking violin and cello and I said, "I'm going to hang out with you guys and we're going to goof off in this class." So I played the viola. We would all go into separate little rooms to figure out scales. We were just banging on the walls and being goofballs; you know, it was seventh grade. When we would play a song, I had to learn it all by ear. I never learned the keys or any sort of notes. I learned everybody's part. In the orchestra, everybody's separate – there's a cello, there's a viola, there's a violin. I didn't know any different, so I just played everyone's part. When the teacher thought that everyone was learning separate parts, she would make everyone play their part solo. When it came to me, I was playing this weird melody. She asked me, "Do you even know what you're doing?" Because I would have the music upside down on purpose, to make my friends laugh. My teacher said, "I don't know what to do with you. You wasted time here, but in a way you didn't because you listened to everything and it's just strange." To this day, I like doing music and I've been in a couple of bands.

Wong's instincts for music were strong enough to win over his teacher, but his talents for art were even more striking.

I found that I would do my art and everyone was very impressed by it. They would have me do yearbook illustrations. A lot of my teachers said things like, "You don't have to do this class. You passed because you're just going to be an artist when you grow up, and you're going to be successful. I have a brother-in-law making a restaurant; can you do the illustrations for the menus?" In some classes, they'd put me in another room and they'd tell me, "Just draw pictures and do whatever you want to do, because this is what you're going to do." Throughout my entire schooling, I think I only wrote three term papers. Then I got a full scholarship to go to art school . . . which I stupidly declined.

Documentarian **Steven Okazaki** was also treated in a different way because of his artistic talents. "From third grade through high school, I drew and painted all the time," he told us.

Students and teachers liked what I did and pegged me as an "artist." People who can't draw think it's magical. "How did you do that?" Like you pulled a rabbit out of a hat. That made me feel special. But it made me more introverted, because I didn't trust it. An amateur magician might get a lot of attention from their friends and family, but what does it amount to?

In the 1950s and 60s culture, there was this romantic notion of artistic people being emotionally fragile. You know, like Van Gogh or Modigliani. I loved art, I ditched school to go to the art museum to stare at paintings by Henri Matisse, Egon Schiele, Renoir, Dürer, Klimt. And when I got in trouble and my parents found out, they didn't get mad. My mother said, "You probably learned more there than in a day at school." I appreciated that, it gave me permission to follow my own path. But I also took advantage of it – the freedom and privileges that went with it – and it separated me from what other kids were doing. I wasn't special. I was just stubborn about my right to be different. That's why I'm so grateful I found filmmaking. You have to do the work, you can't fake it, you can't get by on reputation or mystique. The work has to stand on its own.

Taking Matters into Their Own Hands

Photographer/lighting programmer **Rachael Saltzman** was so bored in her tiny school that she eventually sought out ways to amuse herself, including taking on extra classwork.

Kindergarten through twelfth grade was all in the same building, with a whopping total of 600 students. My graduating class was 52, so there was always that "sore thumb" issue. There were very few facilities. My advanced art class was five teenagers using construction paper, crayons, and this ancient egg tempera. I still remember the odd, mushroomy smell that came from the black paint; I think it had been there as long as my teacher and had all these strange lumps and separations that had to be stirred out (the paint, not my teacher). From Day One, I was often bored and "acted out," as they liked to call it, in all sorts of nonviolent ways. One was my wardrobe. I was perfectly capable of dressing myself when I was young; however, the results were often rather notable. My mother was wise enough not to argue with a five-year-old who decided that purple corduroys, an orange t-shirt, seven bits of costume jewelry, three ponytails, and a teddy bear stashed under her hat was the height of fashion. When I got older, I'd wear my dad's castoffs rather than be bothered spending my own money on something so trivial as clothing, although I did succumb to style from time to time. I remember in high school wearing this godawful faux snow-leopard full-length coat from the 1970s, and long johns that I'd dyed or painted myself.

Being in class itself was torture, and I was in mild trouble constantly. I drew all over the desks, didn't pay attention, and finished all assignments within a couple of minutes. I made a crossbow out of a pencil, paper clip, and rubber band to shoot balls of paper at people (not spitballs – I thought that was gross). With a combination of another pencil, rubber band, and patience, I made a set of pliers and took all the bolts out of my desk.

In second grade, I figured out a way to make the assignments last a bit longer and entertain myself. For about three months, I handed in all assignments in mirror writing, which took me a bit longer than writing normally. My teacher called my mom to have a special meeting where I was also present. My mom asked me to write her a note about the situation, which was, of course, written normally. They had a little powwow over what to do next, and my teacher asked if I would like to read another set of books – of my choice – on top of the regular class work. This was an agreeable compromise, and she graded extra work from me, which is amazing dedication. Sometimes I wish I had them, since I can't help but wonder what an essay about *Fahrenheit 451* from a seven-year-old looks like. I wrote and organized "plays" with some of my classmates, brought in all sorts of things for show and tell – the dead bee and live turtles went over well, even though the turtles got out of their milk crate over the course of the day (the ensuing chaos was also a great hit amongst the three-foot-tall crowd). I'd bring costumes and props from home to put on the plays in class when I was allowed to.

Actress **Donna Lynne Champlin** did not get out of classwork nor add additional assignments, but she was able to use her creativity to improve her grades. "In non-creative subjects, I remember certain teachers allowed me to use my creativity to do extra credit," she said.

I was terrible with remembering actual dates and specifics, but I could easily comprehend all the strategies, the whys, wherefores, and personalities involved. Once, in an American history class, I had studied my brains out for a big test on the triangle trade and was hoping and praying for it to be mostly essay questions. It was all multiple choice. Multiple choice tests were the worst for me because I could overthink almost every answer into being correct in some way. So, I bombed it. I had a great teacher though, and for extra credit I created a diary of a slave on one of the trade ships that documented their first-person experience as a victim of the triangle trade. I still have it somewhere. I had a blast doing it. I even created my own quill pen from a feather and baked all the pages in the oven after dunking them in milk to age them – and I pulled my grade back up.

Of course, sometimes artists aren't only treated differently; they're treated worse. Many people shared stories of individual teachers and broken systems, as we shall soon see.

5 | *School Struggles*
Some of my teachers were almost obstacles

Many people think that schools hurt creativity, even though – it is important to add – there is much less scientific support for this view (e.g., Karwowski, 2021). In general, teachers want to nurture their creative students (e.g., Gregerson et al., 2013). Unfortunately, however, there are some notable exceptions. Photographer/lighting programmer **Rachael Saltzman**'s experiences, for instance, were the stuff of nightmares. "The memories of K-12 are soft enough now, but if I woke up tomorrow and found myself back there, I'd jump off a cliff," she told us.

Things pretty much went to hell in junior high. I have nothing but love for my old math and science instructors, who did the best they could with the gaggles of demons infesting their classrooms. The others, though, pandered to the popular kids, which reinforced their screwed-up behavior. My English teacher's first assignment was that awful "Summer Vacation" essay. My summers were spent in a campground at a fantasy-based Renaissance Festival. One of our tent neighbors was this great guy named Mark, who dressed up as a faun, complete with fuzzy legs and goat horns. I wrote an essay about waking up and getting ready for the day. It was the first assignment I'd ever failed. My teacher conceded that it was well written with no spelling or grammar errors, but that the assignment was not fiction. So she failed me. I came home in tears. My mom was livid, but the teacher refused to listen to her and the grade stayed. I stopped writing for pleasure for a long time.

The art teacher was worse. He was extremely lecherous toward young girls. I begged out sick until my mom noticed that I was trying to stay home on particular days. When she asked, I pleaded not to be forced to go to art class. Since art had been my first love since birth, she knew something was wrong and finally got the story out of me. The art teacher actually tried to tell my mom I had the "vapors" and was making up stories. I stopped doing anything art-related, again, for a long time. Two months into this mess, I stopped talking entirely. I didn't speak again for five years.

Too Creative for School

There are many reasons aside from genuinely evil teachers that might lead to an artist finding school stifling. Novelist **Piers Anthony** talks about the variety of hurdles that he experienced. "I had trouble schooling," Anthony told us.

It took me three years to make it through first grade, and I understand intelligence tests rated me as subnormal. Theoretically, intelligence is constant through life, so how did I go from subnormal to supernormal? Well, there were reasons. I suspect I was dyslexic, as my daughter was, but I learned to compensate. I was always slow, not in the sense of stupid, but in the sense of a locomotive in a drag race with race cars: It's a loser, but put it on a 3,000-mile track and it will show its merit. Life is a long track. I suspect my old high school doesn't care to ponder how I could graduate in the third quarter of my class yet become perhaps the most successful member of that class. Square pegs are not much valued in school.

Another reason was that, when I was tested, it was presented as a game. The answers were so obvious that I couldn't believe that was the point, and gave alternative answers. When I got older, I gave straighter answers, and scored better, though every so often in high school and college I was torpedoed by giving a correct answer instead of a keyed answer. Professors just didn't understand. I suspect IQ tests tend to miss the smartest folk for that reason: They are smarter than the makers of the test, or may simply have a different perspective. I can give examples: "When lost in a forest, how do you find your way out?" Well, I have been lost in a forest, and the keyed answers don't work. I just kept going until I stumbled on a road, then followed that. Climb a tall tree to look around? All you see is more trees. Study the moss at the base of trees, which will be on the north side? No, it isn't; it is determined by shading, wind, and other factors, north being only one. I have seen moss entirely encircling a tree trunk. And what good is it to know where north is, when you don't know where you are? North of lost is still lost. Sometimes I showed my contempt for such misinformation, which surely cost me IQ points. I think my favorite is one others encountered: "Which is the closest planet?" No, it's not Mars. But you can't answer unless you rephrase. If you ask, "What is the closest *orbit*?" then you get Venus. Even then, the question is ridiculous. The closest planet is *Earth*, so close you can literally touch it. But answering literally gets you no points from ignorant test makers. Once I took a speed-reading course, and did not do well. I took the keyed answers to the instructor and pointed out where they were wrong. She admitted it; it turned out to be a bad key. The funny thing was that I was the first to catch it. Others had been giving perfect answers according to that key, making better scores. So I stayed with slow reading, preferring reality to scoring. Then there's the one about the coffee and tea cups – enough, I think I have made my point. I was never stupid, I simply tested that way. In my day, high IQ, like other measures, was largely for conformists; I hope testing has improved in the last half-century or so.

Incidentally, although IQ testing has had its ups and downs, there have been improvements (including those made by James's parents, Alan and Nadeen Kaufman). "In any event, intelligence is only one part of the intellect," Anthony told us.

There is artistry, which is difficult to measure (after eight years of art courses in high school and college I gave it up because in my own judgment I was not good enough to make it as a commercial artist, so I made words my art instead) and, of course, creativity. My greatest strengths are largely unmeasurable – surely a comforting thought for anyone.

Anthony's struggles were systemic in nature, from an educational emphasis on speediness to tests aimed at the lowest common denominator. What often makes for the most striking memories, however, are the individual teachers who are bad apples. Some stand out for their emphasis on rules at the expense of learning.

Asking Questions Can Create Problems

"I asked questions very, very early in my life," writer/producer **Deborah Pratt** told us.

I was raised Catholic and I recall in my first-grade catechism class – I was maybe seven years old – listening to the teacher talk about purgatory and how unbaptized children could never go to heaven, only to purgatory. I raised my hand and asked, "Why would God do that to somebody who didn't even know that this God or Jesus existed? Why would innocent children be sent to purgatory – people who couldn't achieve or hold sight of the most beautiful being, according to your doctrine, who existed in the universe?" I got sent to the school office where the head nun called my parents to come and take me home.

It's not always asking questions that gets you into trouble; sometimes it is having your own artistic style. Writer **Susan Breen** told us how, when her mother sent her to a creative writing camp, the supportive gesture backfired.

I did not want to go because I did not consider myself one of the artistic kids. They dressed differently, with outlandish clothes, and I was quiet and an observer and did not want to be the center of attention. We had to write stories and every one I wrote ended sadly – like someone invariably died at the end. A counselor said to me, "Can't you come up with a happy ending?" I just remember failing at creative writing camp because I could not come up with a happy ending. It was only a week, but I remember saying to my mother, "I hate this camp." Poor thing, my mother was just trying to be supportive.

There are some teachers who are obsessed with any rule-breaking, and then there are the teachers who bend the rules for some but not others. Actress **Donna Lynne Champlin** said,

I ran into trouble with less understanding teachers who had no problem letting a bunch of jocks out of class for a game. But when I had an artistic competition, rehearsal, or show during the day, I would get endless grief and no help in making up the work or tests I'd missed. I'd either have to take the academic hit or ask my mom to call the principal to try to convince them not to penalize me for doing what the jocks were allowed to do.

Personality Clashes

Sometimes the issue is less to do with rules and more to do with personality conflicts. It can be particularly frustrating when the person tasked with teaching the arts is the one who is stifling creativity. Novelist **Diana Abu-Jaber** told us,

Some of my teachers were almost obstacles to overcome when it came to creativity. I had one teacher in particular who was just a nightmare. She didn't have any feeling for children or teaching. She really shouldn't have been a teacher. We were all really scared of her. And she was the art teacher! Which was such a shame. She was the person who should have been so much fun for us, but that's how it was. And I'm sorry to say I don't think much has changed since then.

"I stopped taking piano lessons when I was ten," playwright **John Patrick Bray** remembered.

At first, I had a wonderful teacher. But then I ended up having a piano instructor who was just awful. She just took the joy out of music entirely. When my brother and I decided to stop playing piano, it broke my father's heart. We were coming home with headaches from piano lessons, and it wasn't any fun anymore. There are great teachers in the world and there are those who probably should have found another occupation. Unfortunately, the woman who taught us shouldn't have been giving lessons. She didn't have the right soul for it, I don't think, or the right temperament. Maybe she was just burnt out. I believe she was approaching retirement. I don't know. I just remember not enjoying that at all.

Stories of unsupportive and just plain bad teachers abound. Some teachers even told their students they would never be able to make a living in their chosen creative field so they should give up such dreams altogether. A few people told us that they had given up on being creative – mostly temporarily – because of what a teacher said or did. Fortunately for all of us, many found their way back to creating beautiful, meaningful, or thought-provoking art. Phew, that was close.

PART II

Discovery

6 | *Sudden Insight*
I knew this was my life

What are the key moments of a young child's life? A toddler's first steps, their first cries of "mama" and "no," their first time boarding the school bus – and, for some, the first glimmer of their life's creative purpose. Just like stories of a child's first words, some moments are fuzzy, whereas others have burning clarity. Some are not moments at all, but rather winding paths with both triumphs and a few wrong turns along the way. And, sometimes, people feel as though they have always known what creative work they were meant to do.

Actor **Michael Kostroff**, for instance, has always known. "I was an actor from the get-go," he said.

I don't remember a moment when I didn't want to perform or create stories. I didn't know that that made me different from anybody. I thought that that was the game that everybody wanted to play; I didn't know it was a potential career. I remember making up songs and making everybody watch while I performed them, jumping up and down on the couch. Performing was my catnip. It was those things that made me go, "Yes, yes, yes, I want that." They all had to do with making things up. It wasn't the attention, so much – it was the stepping into other characters' lives that grabbed me from the beginning. I did go through a period, around eighteen years old, when I wondered whether I wanted to do the arts for a living because I knew how difficult it was and how crazy people in the arts were. So, I worked in a bank, I paid my rent, and I just floundered for a bit. At a certain point, I realized that being an actor, for me, was as inherent to who I am as my hair color or my eye color or anything else about me and I made a very important decision. I decided that even if I pursued it and had no success at all, I would still be fulfilling my own destiny and my design. That was an important turning point for me. I just realized that in order to be an authentic Michael Kostroff, I had to be an actor.

Painter **Shanee Epstein**, like Kostroff, has always been aware that she sees the world through an artist's eyes. "Art and being an artist is the earliest part of my identity that I can remember," she told us.

I was always doing art projects. I did a lot of clay work because my uncle was a potter. I also built caterpillar homes. I was always making things. It was very natural to me, like athletes must on some level feel an urge to move. I love color and I became kind of obsessed with it. I see it very brightly, very intensely. I'm very affected by my surroundings and by the aesthetics and what things look like and what things feel like, and I think that translates on an emotional level. I remember taking tons of pictures of just color combinations, like colors near each other. Years later, I decided to let go of everything else and went back to basics – to let go of line, to let go of shape, and just study color for three years. I had two shows on it, just myself, with paintings about studying color.

Writer **Tess Gerritsen**'s calling was for the written word, though she worked as a medical doctor for years. "I always knew I was going to be a writer," she said.

Maybe it would be just as a hobby, but I knew I was going to write. I wrote my first book when I was seven years old. It was a biography of my dead cat and I bound it myself, with a needle and thread to make it look as much like a book as I could. I progressed eventually to writing on cloth because I realized that paper was going to tear. I still have a bound book that I made for my brother for his birthday, with illustrations. Bad illustrations, but the story was there.

Other creators can pinpoint the exact moment they fell in love with creativity. For actor-writer **Jim Piddock**, the realization of what he wanted to do came with a jolt. "I did a play at school," he told us, "and I remember standing in the wings just before my first entrance in the first show, thinking this was the most terrified I'd ever been in my entire life – and I was going to do this for the rest of my life. It was an immediate addiction to adrenaline. I actually like the adrenaline side of it less now."

Photographer **Greg Friedler**'s artistic passion began with a present from his father. It came as he neared adulthood. "I didn't take photographs until I was seventeen years old," he told us.

When I left home to go to boarding school, my dad gave me his Olympus OM-1 camera, a basic 35 mm, and said, "I think you'll like it." That is what started everything. From the second I picked up that camera, I was obsessed. None of the photography classes felt like classes. I pursued it with reckless abandon. The first photo I took was just a landscape and it was to figure out how the camera worked and F-stops and shutter speeds and all that stuff. Four months later, they assigned me to take a portrait for the first time. They didn't say how to do it. I don't remember doing it, but I remember the outcome. I knocked it out of the park. I took an amazing portrait of a kid who was in my dorm. It was composed well and framed well and the lighting was good. My teacher sent a letter to my parents, saying that he thought there was something strange going on because he hadn't seen anyone take a picture like that who had never taken a portrait before. But I had no clue what I was doing. I was just pointing the camera.

Creativity Teams

Friends and family often serve as entryways to the arts. For writer **Dara Horn**, artistic awakening came when she and her best friend invented complex worlds and told engaging stories set within these worlds. "When I was going into first grade," she said,

I became very close friends with a girl in my class who was a very creative person. We created our own solar system. We had our own comets and there was a fly, named Time Flies, that went from one planet to another. Each planet had different traits. One was a rainbow planet that was covered with rainbow clouds, and you could hide there in the shadows. We lived on the snow planet, which was always covered with snow. There was another planet that was a mud planet. We each had a character that we played and we would go to these different planets and have adventures. There was an enemy we were fighting; it was an elaborate Dungeons & Dragons kind of thing, except that we generated all the material ourselves. We'd play the game for like an hour and we would keep a journal of everything that happened in the game. It was called a journal, but we were documenting imaginary events. The girl I played with is still my closest friend. I don't know how much we influenced each other or whether we were just fortunate to find each other. She probably influenced me; I don't know if I influenced her at all.

Incidentally, Horn's childhood playmate and creative co-conspirator, Elif Batuman, has written several books, including the Pulitzer Prize-nominated novel *The Idiot*.

Playwright **John Patrick Bray**'s early co-creating experiences were with his brother, Gregg. "When my brother and I were in third grade, we started writing poetry," he said.

We gave our poems to all the other kids and we had them sign up for which poems they wanted. We had fans. We would write all these things mostly about bears and animals and what have you and pass them out. And we had a great time with that. If I had to trace the writing bug back to a moment, it would be passing out poetry in the third grade.

Seeking Peer Support

As the Bray brothers discovered, support from friends can be a powerful motivator. The positive attention muralist **David Guinn** received from his peers helped nudge him toward his art. "I got onto an academic track in high school," he told us, "so I didn't take any art classes. But I started painting t-shirts that I would wear, which was a way of individuating myself. I liked the attention that I got from artwork, from making t-shirts. I was basically using the tee shirt as a canvas and then I would wear it."

Lyricist-librettist **Bill Russell** also found that his creativity – writing, in his case – brought him the admiration of his peers. He told us:

I grew up in the Black Hills of South Dakota and my paternal grandparents were cattle ranchers in Wyoming, just over the border, so I spent a lot of time out at their ranch. But for some reason, I was bitten by the theater bug really early on. When I was in second grade, I organized all my friends and I wrote and directed a production of *Cinderella*. A lot of kids do that, but what was different about me was I talked all the teachers in the elementary school into letting out class to see my show. Then I started writing poetry when I was in high school. I was very inspired by e e cummings. Plus, I was in love with this friend of mine, this guy. I wrote all this love poetry to him, not even acknowledging to myself that I was gay. It was just love. It wasn't explicitly love poetry for him; it was couched in metaphor. He had transferred to my high school for his senior year and that was during my junior year. He was leaving at the end of the year and, for graduation, I gave him a book of all the stuff I'd written about him. We didn't go into the underlying implications. He just appreciated the creativity and uniqueness of it.

Singer **Country Joe McDonald** discovered that his art not only brought him peer support but also gave him an amount of political power, for better or worse. He said:

My parents were left-wing politically so there was a lot of left-wing political music in my house. Mainstream people would only recognize Woody Guthrie and Pete Seeger, but there were a lot of other people who sang topical songs. In addition to the rhythm and blues and jazz and stuff, I had topical songs. I'd written a song about a spaceship coming to earth, a rock and roll novelty tune, and my friend who was running for class president asked me to perform it at an assembly. I changed the last wording of the song to say, "Vote for him for president." And he got elected. So, I think that was probably my first discovery of the power of political song and how it can influence people. He wasn't the person who should have been president at all. He was a football player. But he did get elected.

But peer support can be a double-edged sword. Actress **Donna Lynne Champlin** remembered when, early on, she had to balance the thrill of peer approval – in the form of applause – with the best interests of the artwork itself:

My first recognition that I was consciously being creative, along the lines of taking an impulsive liberty from the norm as I knew it, would have to be when I was six and got my first laugh onstage. I was playing Gretl in *The Sound of Music*. In the second act, we were saying goodbye and exiting on our way to escape offstage. I passed a Nazi and made a "Goodbye-yai-yai!" joke without realizing what I was actually doing. It just ... happened. I believe the phrase "taking creative license" applied. I had no idea up until that point in my life that I even had a sense of humor. There were a lot of discoveries for me in that one moment. It got a huge laugh, which thrilled me no end. Not to mention the feeling of power to be a little girl and make hundreds of people react.

But the director, of course, was furious. It couldn't have been more wrong and inappropriate to the storytelling. She chewed me out after the show, and rightly so. As an actor, my job was to take direction and do the part as we had rehearsed. I was warned that, if I ever did that again, I would be fired. I remember walking to the car through the parking lot with my mom after the director had yelled at me; my mom had been there the whole time and let the director yell without stepping in because there was no denying I deserved it. I was in tears. I had become intoxicated with the experience of impulsively creating something that was my own, and then getting hundreds of people to laugh. I didn't want to let it go. I wanted to see if I could do it again. Not recreate it, but to create it again. But I also understood that I would get into tremendous trouble if I did. I asked my mom what I should do, and she totally left it up to me. We discussed actions and consequences, and whether I understood why the director was so mad. She told me that, ultimately, the choice came down to doing what I felt was right. In the end, I opted not to go for the laugh. I always loved my mother for not stepping in when I was getting yelled at and for letting me make the call as to what was right in that moment and what wasn't – and why.

Having a strong idea of what you want to do from childhood can provide a level of focus, clarity, and ambition that can often lead to success. We have seen these connections in many of the artists' experiences described in this chapter. But there can also be advantages to taking a more circuitous route to your chosen creative field, as we will explore in the next chapter.

7 | Specific Inspiration
I practiced what I heard on the radio

Some young artists stumble across their inspiration when they experience another person's work. Early encounters with theater, television shows, movies, books, and music can serve as catalysts for a lifetime in the arts. At the most fundamental level, experiencing art can demonstrate that such a form is possible. And that maybe, just maybe, you can make a living that way.

Writer-musician **Cecil Castellucci** had their magic epiphany when they first encountered a galaxy far, far away:

The moment that I knew for sure that telling stories was what I wanted to do, absolutely – when it all sort of jelled – was when I saw *Star Wars*. At the end of the movie, when Darth Vader goes spinning off because they blew up the Death Star, I understood that there might be another movie and that it might be somebody's job to make up what would happen next. And I thought, "That's the job I want. I want to write the next *Star Wars*." Before then, stories were always the biggest deal in my life, but it wasn't a thing I thought I could do. Once I decided that that was what I was going to do, there's never been any deviation from me wanting to be a storyteller. Ever.

Castellucci's many projects include a graphic novel in the official *Star Wars* series, *Moving Target: A Princess Leia Adventure*.

Writer **David Morrell** was inspired to pursue a life in writing by a television show. "*Route 66* was the show that made me want to be a writer," he told us.

I was seventeen when it premiered, and it spoke to me in ways that still affect me all these years later. The show was about two young men in a Corvette convertible who have nothing except the car. Family tragedies have left them orphans, so without ties, they set off down the road to find out what America is. The show was filmed entirely on location, wherever they happened to be in the story. If they pulled in in St. Louis, then it was filmed in St. Louis. It had a wonderful jazz score by Nelson Riddle, a new one every week. Stirling Silliphant, who won the Oscar for *In the Heat of the Night*, wrote most of the episodes. All of them were about searching, looking forward, finding your way; it really affected me. When I watched *Route 66,* I knew my destiny was to be a writer. Stirling's scripts made me want to be him. There was no looking back; the rest of my life became arranging what I needed to do to have that career happen.

Dancer-psychologist **Paula Thomson** remembered, "My first moment discovering my passion for dance was as a small child, around five years old. I saw the ballet *Swan Lake,* and after that experience I knew I wanted to dance. I walked to school like a ballerina swan for weeks after witnessing that performance."

Musician **Bruce Mack**'s love of the arts began early and kept growing as he learned of its many possibilities. "I could sort of see the sound a little bit," he said.

I couldn't play any instruments, but I could see the sound sort of like colors. I knew I wanted to be a part of sound. I could hear horns; I always loved horns. I auditioned for the school band in fourth grade and got in to play baritone horn. From that point until seventh grade, my family moved around a lot, so I wasn't able to spend enough time in a school to get settled in a music program. The next thing I knew, I was in junior high school with a group of kids who'd been playing for years already. They had all kinds of facility, they could just play! I knew I had something in me, but I wasn't at their level. By the time I was in high school, I started singing with a vocal group, a cappella doo-wop. If I could hear it, I could sing it. I felt I had the voice because I could mimic horn solos. In the vocal groups we wrote a couple songs, but sang more covers, imitating groups like the Chi-Lites, Blue Magic, the Stylistics, and others. My older sister Delores and the parent of one of the vocal group members would make our outfits and we'd play around town for money. We had regular rehearsal schedules, we knew what we were doing. We'd play at schools, community centers, audition and do talent shows around the city. We ran our own little business and raised money for churches.

Becoming musically independent was the culmination of having to move around and not really being able to develop my abilities on an instrument between the ages of eight and fifteen. I think those formative years of development continue into this period of one's life, especially if there are specific interests. When I was fourteen, I listened to a lot of records. I'd go to record shops and see magazines about music, flip through pages and read about stuff that wasn't on the radio. I got exposed to lots of alternative stuff and knew where to find it. Around that time, FM radio had come about and I started hearing stuff I had read about by listening to disc jockeys who played artists considered underground. That was my beginning of being creative: listening to music, finding out who created it, and hearing all the nuances. Sometimes I get upset that I didn't have the chance to develop musically at a young age, but you know, I have the chance to do it now. I've taught myself several instruments since then – bass, percussion, keyboards.

Switching Creative Gears

Even when an artist moves away from the art form that inspired them as a child, it may still influence their work. Librettist **Michael Colby's** love of comic books played an indirect role in his musical theater success. He recalled:

Coupled with musical theater, comic books were another major source of inspiration for me. I wrote and illustrated a bunch of homemade comic books, stories that I made up like short graphic novels. While other kids were busy with sports, I had a geek outlet; I saw myself in terms of super-heroes. I always say that I started my career writing letters to Superman Comics and I had a lot of them published. If you Google "Michael Colby" and "Superman," you'll see old letters I wrote as a kid. It's kind of crazy, like a ghost has come back from the past. A lot of my musicals have that same fantasy quality.

Similarly, writer-producer **Chris Bearde** rediscovered the joy of comedy while pursuing a different art form. "After I left high school, I went to an art college," he told us.

I skipped the art classes, especially the boring ones like lettering ... So I would sneak off and watch Charlie Chaplin and all those guys in the silent movies. I started laughing at these guys and going hysterical. It was like, "Oh my god, that's so great. I think I'd rather do that than this." Of course, people who go to college sometimes find that they don't want to do their subject; they want to do something else. But at least they're at a place where they can do something else. I was learning more about slapstick comedy than I was about art. Painting was this still thing. I wanted movement.

Sometimes, insights into the creative life come in two parts. First, someone realizes that such an art form exists and appreciates its wonder; second, they realize that they actually could be part of that world. Singer-songwriter **Julie Gold** remembered:

For my fourth birthday, my parents took me to see *My Fair Lady*. My father was not an athletic person, but he still dug the car out of the snow and drove downtown. We had dinner at Horn & Hardart. My brother and I were nice, well-behaved, cute kids and these glamorous women came over to our table. My father said, "These are my children, this is Julie, and it's her birthday – we're seeing *My Fair Lady*." They said, "We're in the chorus. Where will you be seated?" In those days, my parents would buy two orchestra seats and two balcony seats. One of them would sit with one of us in the orchestra and the other would sit with the other one in the balcony. Then we'd switch at intermission so everybody could see everything: the orchestra, the distance, the whole thing. My father told them where we would be in the orchestra and that I would be seated there for Act Two. I know now that they couldn't have seen us – it's too dark when you're onstage. But when the bows were taken, the ladies waved to us. *My Fair Lady* is one of the greatest, greatest shows of all time. The greatest music ever written. It grabbed me by the throat. To this day, if I put it on, I'll start crying my eyes out. It changed my life and it was like magical dust was thrown on me. The whole next day and the day after, I cried my eyes out. I missed everyone so much. My mother called my father at work and he explained that it's a show, they're actors, and they do it every night of the week. He said, "I'll take you for the rest of your life, any time you want to go." It was all part of the revelation that there's this whole world out there that involves music as an art form.

I was six when I started piano and I took it until twelfth grade. I thought I was going to stay with classical and pursue it. That's all I was learning. It wasn't until I was a pre-teenager that pop music entered my life and unlocked this question: Where does it come from? Somebody makes this music, somebody writes this music. Like if you bought a 45-rpm record, it would say the Beatles, with Lennon and McCartney in parentheses. Who were Lennon and McCartney? Who were Burt Bacharach and Hal David? Who were these mysterious names? Well, they wrote, wrote, wrote, wrote the song. The song just doesn't happen, it's created. And then I thought, "Well, what makes a songwriter? Can anybody do it?" Until you try, you don't know. Everybody thinks they can write a song. But most people shouldn't. When I started branching out in the ninth grade and writing songs, my piano teacher asked, "Did you practice this week? Because you don't seem like you practiced." No, I was at the piano for hours and hours and hours, but no, I did not practice my lesson. I practiced what I heard on the radio. But how do you tell your piano teacher that? She would write, "Don't forget to practice." I was prepared enough for my lessons and it's not like my parents saw my piano lessons as the be-all and end-all. If I'd said, "Mom and Dad, I'm not getting anything out of this anymore," they would have said, "Okay. You did great. Hopefully, it will follow you the rest of your life." But when I started playing and writing pop songs, I knew that was what I was going to do. Period.

Finding Identity through Creativity

Actor **Doug Jones** fell in love with television early on, but he needed to see someone who looked like him on screen before he could envision such a future for himself. "I'd get home from school," he said,

the TV would go on, and I would escape – not into kids' programming, but into more adult programming like sitcoms and variety shows. I just loved them and absorbed them. Like reruns of *I Love Lucy* and the *Dick Van Dyke Show* and the *Mary Tyler Moore Show* and *Bob Newhart* – oh my gosh, the *Carol Burnett Show*. I never missed an episode. And then there were all the other variety shows; Donny and Marie Osmond and Tom Jones and everybody had variety shows. I got into escape: song and dance, comedic sketches, or the sitcoms where families would deal with their issues and hug each other by the end of the half hour. That was the world I wanted to be a part of. And I found myself getting very close, almost friends with these characters I was watching on TV. Barney Fife of *The Andy Griffith Show* was a very early inspiration for me – a skinny, goofy guy who also had a sense of humor about himself. Don Knotts was just a genius. I thought, "See, there is a place for skinny, goofy people who have a big bottom lip. I can see it right there." So that gave me the idea that I wanted to be in that TV box one day. That's where these people lived. I wanted to be with them.

Seeing a star who looks like you can help affirm that you belong and can succeed. Such aspirational role models in the arts can be even more important for those who are a member of an underrepresented group (Charland, 2010). Sometimes, just one artist who shares your background can be enough to demonstrate that you can find a home in what had once seemed to be an exclusive club. Playwright **Kristoffer Diaz** remembers:

A play by John Leguizamo called *Spic-O-Rama* changed my life in high school. It was a one-man show where he played six people from his family. It was brilliant and knocked me out. It was the first time I had really seen a Latino family onstage that could have been me and my cousins and people who I could have known. And I thought, "Oh, I get this." These are different characters who could be based on people in Leguizamo's life but they could also be based on different aspects of his own personality. It was clear to me exactly what he was doing, and I wanted to do something like that. It was funny, it was Latino, it had some hip-hop influence. It was so different. A lot of plays are about rich White people sitting on a couch, drinking wine, and talking about whether they're going to sell the family house or find a job.

I can't watch that. It's so outside of my experience. There was no place in the conversation for me. I felt connected to every single moment of Leguizamo's work. It changed my expectations.

Over time, Diaz's views have evolved.

This type of play is still my favorite, but as I've gotten older, purchased a home, and been exposed to more folks from different backgrounds, I've gained more of an appetite for work outside my experience. I've even written a "rich folks sitting in a house drinking wine" play (called *Things with Friends*), though I'm intentionally messing with that convention a bit in that piece. The guts of this are still true; John's work changed everything for me.

Experiencing and enjoying other people's art can also be a way to develop your own creativity. The act of replicating and putting your own spin on an idea you like (whether by design or unintentionally) can be a natural part of the creative process (Sternberg et al., 2002). Literary scholar **Aviva Briefel** remembered:

I must have been in second grade when I wrote a story for my English class about a made-up society in which things were different from our own. My teacher singled out one detail from my story as being particularly creative: Instead of record players, the people in my imagined society used birds to play records. The birds would drop their beaks on a rotating disk, and the friction would produce music. My teacher was impressed, called me creative, and asked me to read this passage out loud to the class. My classmates, on the other hand, were less impressed because they recognized the image of the bird and the record player: "Hey, that's from the *Flintstones*." If you've ever watched the cartoon, you probably had the same reaction – the image of the bird record player is about as familiar as the car that runs on foot power. I hadn't meant to plagiarize this image; it was just one of the things floating in my mind while writing the story. One could make the case that my particular use of this image was original, given the surrounding context. But I find it interesting that, because my teacher didn't have the same knowledge base and points of reference as my classmates, *this* is what he identified as creative.

Incidentally, this is a concept Briefel continues to think about; her first book was *The Deceivers: Art Forgery and Identity in the Nineteenth Century*.

Novelist **Susan Choi** also started off, in part, by reinterpreting existing works. "As a kid," she told us,

I wrote stories and I liked writing plagiarized versions of my favorite books that I imagined were really original. I was a big reader as a kid. I started writing stories at a really early age, but I didn't understand how to write original stories at all. I would get inspired by an idea and then just copy it with a slight change. For example, my favorite books for a time were *The Borrowers* series by Mary Norton, about people who were about a foot tall. So I wrote a series of stories about the Pinheads, who were little, short people who were a couple inches tall.

Cristina García ended up as a writer, but her early replicating experiences were in the visual arts. "I loved to paint as a kid and I thought that's what I would do," she said. "Mostly, I liked to paint reproductions of things. I would try to paint what I saw in a postcard or a magazine and then make it my own. I got tremendous satisfaction painting something similar but changing it in significant ways. I guess I was having authorial impulses even then."

Artistic passions can be ignited in many ways: a sudden spark, a long and winding fuse, or an extension of an existing conflagration. But regardless of how the blaze begins, it's interesting to see how the process continues. The life of an artist can proceed as straightforwardly or as roundabout as it begins, as we see in the next chapter.

8 The Winding Path
I was a Renaissance kid

Childhood is a time for exploration, and many young artists try their hand at a variety of creative forms. Even those who have always known their passion may dabble a bit. For example, actor-writer-record producer **Bruce Kimmel** has always been an entertainer, though his precise choice of outlet has varied over the years. "I was very affected by movies as a child," he told us.

I created my own worlds. I made a camera out of the cardboard from my father's laundered shirts and would walk around the neighborhood, holding my "camera" as if I were a TV host. I wanted to be an actor from the time I can remember. I did death scenes at parties, where I would sort of fall on the ground and lie there the entire party. Stuff like that. I sang a lot. I pounded the piano. I didn't know how to play, but that didn't stop me. I was always in love with music and acting and this idea of being on TV. I used to lie in bed pretending that I was being filmed by a VistaVision camera. So, yes, I had an active fantasy life as a child.

In the tenth grade, instead of banging at the piano, I actually started writing melodies. I had never taken piano lessons and my mother said, "If you're going to bang, I'm going to have someone come in." She found a teacher. After I took six months of piano, I wrote a song called "I'm in Like with You," an expression I used with girls. The melody came, the words came, it took like five minutes. I wrote another song and another song. When I discovered theater, I was sort of incorrigible. We would have dinner every Monday night for family members and I did my little Bruce Kimmel Hour, where I did impressions and sang. I don't know if it was good, but they were tolerant. *West Side Story* was my favorite movie in junior high. I did everything I could from that movie: dancing, singing, wearing the clothes. I remember bringing a switchblade to school because I thought it was like *West Side Story*. It wasn't with the intent to harm. It was with the intent to go da-da-da-da-da-bam. They knew it. They did not send me home, they did not take it away from me; they just said it's best not to bring that back.

Likewise, librettist **Michael Colby** has been driven to entertain for as long as he can remember. "I was a Renaissance kid," he said.

I was always kind of creative. I loved to draw, to pretend, to play act, and to write. I remember that, throughout my childhood, I put on marionette shows and wrote theater and did home movies using anyone who would be in them. They were very much in the tradition of slapstick comedy. I was influenced by Ernie Kovacs on television, the sitcoms of my time, and silent film comedies. I used to do caricatures for our schoolbooks, and when someone was running for the student council, I did variations in the style of Al Hirschfeld. I have a whole roomful of paintings I did as a kid that were very much in the style of theatrical posters. These days, the only thing I can draw is maybe a straight line. I was always very poetic. When I was in eighth grade, we were asked to write poetry with onomatopoeia and the different poetry terms; they had people choose up teams and everybody wanted to be on my team. It was the poetry and the writing and the storytelling that just followed me through life, like Peter Pan's shadow.

Creativity is a Hunger

Some children find inspiration in anything and everything. "I was a terror," photographer/lighting programmer **Rachael Saltzman** told us.

Sometimes I still feel for my parents – if I felt like doing something, I'd find a way. If I saw it or thought it, I'd try it. I jumped off the roof of the house with my bedsheet when I was two, because I thought it would make a great parachute. Before that, I'd tried it with an umbrella after seeing *Mary Poppins*. I dismantled our television looking for Kermit the Frog, since I knew he lived in there somewhere. When I grew up, I was going to be Robin Hood. Since my first exposure was the Disney version, that meant I was also going to be an anthropomorphic red fox. To that end, I colored my face with crayons, paints, makeup, whatever was around, so I could be a closer approximation of my idol. One summer, I wanted to go ice skating. Since there would be no ice on the pond for quite a while, I dumped out every bottle of shampoo and conditioner onto the bathroom floor and went skating in my socks. I was insanely curious, and like most kids, would try all sorts of nutty things before learning how. I remember trying to make perfume for my mom by mashing up some flowers from the garden and leaving them in water in an elephant-shaped glass box. About a week later, the stench of rotting plant material got my mom's attention. She was great; after cleaning the mess, she explained to me about essential oils and alcohol, and we tried it the right way.

Every kitchen utensil was a musical instrument. I remember the egg slicer with particular fondness, because it made these great Middle Eastern quarter tone sounds. I was obsessed with trying to figure out how to mix sounds on top of each other on my Fisher-Price tape recorder. I'd record things extra loud, and record over them more quietly with another instrument or singing, making music with five or six different objects. That was about the limit of volume control-based recording for that tape deck. I was about four before I got frustrated with the limitations of the single-track recording method. I had, and still have, a love affair with blank paper. There was no empty page left undrawn or unwritten on. I remember my dad bringing home dot matrix paper from work (with the tear-off holes along the sides) and thinking it was the coolest thing ever. Since the paper was perforated in 8x11 sheets, you could leave them together and make a drawing as long as the whole dining room. It was about that point that I started drawing rudimentary sequential art – comics, if you will. And I was always building something, breaking something and trying to remake it – obsessed with making things that *did* something. With the help of pushpins and glue, a lot of my sculptures at the time had connecting gears, doors that opened, or some sort of interactive element. I was always asking people for stuff I could use to make other things; lobster claws were a biggie, along with bones, scraps of cloth, or anything shiny. Pretty much anything that grabbed my attention would end up being converted into something else.

Saltzman is not the only artist to have a childhood filled with endless curiosity. Novelist **Robert Olen Butler**'s first efforts began in the crib and spanned movies, comic books, and visual art. "One evening," he told us,

when I was a toddler, my mother heard me talking late at night. I was supposed to be asleep. She stepped into the room and found me standing in my crib. She asked me, "What are you doing? What are you talking about?" I told her, "I'm pulling a movie out of the wall." That was the earliest indication of some kind of creative something going on. When I was five or six, I wrote and drew pictures and stapled them together into little de facto comic books. I still have one, *The Hard Bullet*. I loved Westerns; this was the era of Hopalong Cassidy. I remember looking at the pictures I drew with the story. The images in the comic book showed fairly sophisticated use of long shots, close-ups, and various angles. I remember there was a pursuit on horseback and one of the pages, without dialogue, was one of the principals involved in the chase. They're crossing a bridge and what I have drawn is – I can only call it a camera angle from beneath the bridge – so we see the underneath of the horse and the face of the character, shot at a slight angle. It sounds like I was working my way up to be a moviemaker, but I wasn't.

I went on drawing quite a lot. When I was eight years old, I designed a dozen or more automobiles, named them, gave them specifications and so forth. My cars all had tail fins. These pictures have now been lost, but I still have a clear memory of them. This was 1953, and it wasn't until 1957 that Detroit started putting fins on cars. Maybe they stole them, maybe that's where those pictures went. It was a very visual kind of creative childhood. I wrote my first short story when I was eleven years old, during the Korean War. It was called "23 Flights" and it was about this F-86 pilot who had a very difficult dogfight with a couple of MiG-15s from Korea.

Exploring Different Ways of Being Creative

Keith Wong also experimented in a variety of fields when he was growing up. He continues to explore different arenas; he is a visual artist, character designer, and animator who has also drawn comic books, illustrated children's books, and created paintings and sculptures. He remembered,

I drew, I constructed, and I liked making music as a child. I would do comic books, I would create entire sets inside my room. I would make it an entire space station, tear it down and then make it an entire ice cave with sound effects. I learned from a book how to make an audio loop tape and made one of just low wind blowing, as if you were in a cave. I made a bunch of paper mâché stalactites and stuff like that. I was interested in building and creating so I would get refrigerator boxes from behind supermarkets or appliance stores. I would collect diodes and switches and whatnot, and cables that I would hang from the ceiling so it would give it atmosphere. I would have friends come over and we would paint and we would put lights behind switches and I would have reel-to-reel recorders and TVs stuck in as monitors on walls. We would make little movies with Super 8 cameras. I was very interested in the behind-the-scenes stuff. I got many books and magazines about how to make in-camera effects and matte paintings, which they don't use any more; they use all digital stuff now. If you had a Roman Empire movie, sometimes they would paint the top areas or certain sections and place it over the live action, so it looked like there was a giant castle when it was actually just a little oil painting. My friends and I honed our craft by messing around.

Visual artist-entrepreneur **Phyllis Brody**'s many explorations, all centered in arts and crafts, started in early childhood:

When I was a little kid, there was a radio program on Sunday mornings called *Uncle Don*. Parents could send in their child's name and Uncle Don would pick some lucky kids' names and tell those children to look for a surprise. Once, he told *me* to go look under my bed because there was a present for me – and it was a little sewing kit. I remember loving it. Loving the way everything was laid out and had its own place: the needles, the thimble, the fabric, and the embroidery thread. In kindergarten, I remember being given manila paper and folding it in quarters and coloring in each segment for each season. I used to make cards with drawings, poems, and sayings (and still do). From an early age, I liked dimensionality. For my Sweet Sixteen, I made all the centerpieces and party favors with little dolls made out of modeling clay and pipe cleaners and dressed them in crepe paper dresses.

Brody continues to create artwork, often with a three-dimensional element.

For many artists, exploring different domains continues beyond childhood. It is common to refine or switch areas of interest in high school, college, and beyond. When we last heard from playwright **John Patrick Bray,** he had been writing poetry in elementary school with his brother. He continued to co-create with Gregg throughout high school, which helped him find his true passion. "When I was in high school, I took a video class at Dutchess Community College [Poughkeepsie, NY]," he said.

Other students had to put together a short movie and they were having trouble coming up with a script. My brother and I said we could write it, and they gave us the green light. The resulting script was very wordy and longer than they had wanted: seventy minutes instead of maybe twenty. The teacher and other students involved said to us that the script would work much better as a stage play because there were way too many words, too many monologues, for a movie. So, my brother and I said, let's just try this as a play. So, he and I just sat down at the kitchen table and rewrote it. We got it produced a couple of years later when we were full-time students at the same college in 1996. Everybody pitched in – the Programming Board, a local community theater group, our drama club, my parents. It was called *Foul Feast* and we took a video of it. I have trouble watching it now because I don't like watching myself perform. But we thought it was fun and the audience liked it and we felt good about that. That was it. From that moment on, it was like, "I'm a playwright." By the way, my brother and I gave it one more revision a few years ago, had an informal reading, and it is now published with Next Stage Press.

Finding Your Niche

Bray moved toward playwrighting; conversely, novelist **Robert Olen Butler** shifted away from playwrighting. He recalled:

I studied oral interpretation in college, which is a critical approach to literature through performance. It was taken as a premise that all writing, not just literature but all writing, has an implicit persona, a narrative persona. Even your cereal box has a persona. And one can discern and study and then embody in performance the implied emotional characteristics, the personality of that persona. I mean, your cereal box, he's a pretty single-minded guy and he's quite an enthusiast and probably covering a lot of stuff up because you don't get that enthusiastic about corn flakes if there wasn't something else going on under the surface. And so on. You just look at the implications of language, any kind of language strung together by a person, and there is subtext and there is a personality that emerges and with charac-teristics that one can, in oral interpretation, embody in performance.

They allowed me not to write any papers for classes, but to write plays. Because I was interested in the theater, when I realized I wanted to write, my immediate assumption was that I wanted to write plays. In fact, oral inter-pretation is a wonderful training for a fiction writer. Learning how to inhabit a narrative voice that is made up of words is, in essence, the writer's job. But I was really a terrible playwright and I should have known. My most impassioned writing was going into the stage directions, and that's a very bad sign for a playwright. The theater is a collaborative art form. The final art object exists only as a collaborative venture. It doesn't exist in the script, it doesn't exist in the actor's body, it doesn't exist in the stage design, and it doesn't exist in the stage blocking of the bodies. It exists in all of that put together, and my playwriting revealed that I was a closet fiction writer because I felt compelled to control the object I was creating – every lift of the eyebrow, every tone of voice, all the details of the physical space. I eventually came to my senses and realized that fiction was really my medium. Ultimately, the artist does not choose their medium; it chooses them.

Michael Krass knew he wanted to be involved with theater, but didn't immediately realize his niche. It took a while for him to discover that his calling was in costume design:

I went to a very conservative little school, which I hadn't quite realized. I majored in theater. They had a little program with six or seven majors each year which meant that everybody did everything. I had to act and I had to write plays and I had to design lights and I had to direct. That was great, just great. I discovered that I didn't really like acting. I thought I wasn't smart enough to be a director and understand themes in plays and language styling. I was wrong, I just needed to read more. But at that point, I thought, "Oh no, I'm not smart enough to do that." I was a little bored. I had done a lot of scenery in high school and college, designing and painting and building. I thought, "I'm kind of tired of lumber and kind of tired of carpenters, but I do like actors. I should find out about costumes." So I got out of school and I moved to New York and I talked my way into a job at a costume company.

That's my training. I have no training in education and I'm a teacher. I have no training in costumes; I never took a class in costume design. I don't sew. And I'm a costume designer. Hilarious.

Novelist **T. Coraghessan Boyle** also made a few shifts, going from music to history to, ultimately, fiction:

I came to writing late, which is why I love teaching and I love the idea of the liberal arts education. I wanted to be a musician and I went to SUNY Potsdam. I grew up in New York and this is New York's music school. And I flunked my audition. I could play the hell out of my instrument, the saxophone, but I didn't really relate to any of the music we were expected to play and maybe I wasn't as good as some of the others. But there I was at a liberal arts school, so I declared a history major and liked it, as you can see from my novels. I went into a class on the American short story and was literally blown away by Flannery O'Connor, so I did a double major in history and English. Then, in my junior year, I blundered into a creative writing classroom and began to see what I wanted to do. At twenty-two, I finally found what I wanted to do and I went straight for it.

Sports to Arts

Sometimes, people discover the arts after pursuing less obviously related areas. Playwright **Kristoffer Diaz** came to the theater stage from a baseball field. "I was a sports guy first," he told us.

Baseball. My best friend growing up and I, when we weren't playing baseball, would be recreating baseball teams. Or we'd memorize line-ups from different teams and go out and play games as those players and keep track of what happened. I think there's some element of storytelling that was mixed into that. As we got older, we did that a lot with professional wrestling. We'd watch it on television, but we'd also get all these magazines and there'd be names of wrestlers who we hadn't ever heard of, so we'd go by their names or pictures and add them into the stories that we were acting out with our wrestling figures.

When baseball season ended and there were a few weeks before basketball season started, I had nothing to do on a Saturday. I found out there were auditions down at the high school and I thought it was something I was going to want to do. I realized that that's where the girls were. It was either spend my three days a week playing baseball with a bunch of guys or I could spend three days a week rehearsing with a bunch of girls. That was the decision. From there, I think I just started to really enjoy it. I try to avoid it, but that's really the story – I followed the girls. I got into a show and I had like two lines or something in the first show and sort of went from there. It quickly became a lot more satisfying than practicing baseball. But I found that the difference between high school acting and professional acting is the difference between high school football and professional football. It's a completely different kind of skillset and a completely different approach. I don't think that I ever had it in me to really throw myself into acting in the way that most professional actors do. It was never that kind of hugely exciting experience for me. The community of theater was really what I got attracted to. Once I got to college, I started to realize there were a ton of other jobs you could do in the theater – and I think I tried them all out. I studied directing, I studied stagecraft to build sets and things like that. I stumbled into a couple of writing classes and realized that *that* was something that I really enjoyed.

Diaz hasn't forgotten his sports-based roots. Both his play *The Elaborate Entrance of Chad Deity* and the television show *GLOW* are about professional wrestlers.

Writer-performance artist **Annie Lanzillotto** also went from sports to drama. In her case, however, sports were a temporary fallback outlet when theater was unavailable. "In high school, there wasn't any room for any genderbending in drama club," she said.

There wasn't any room. I tried out for the roles, but I didn't get cast. In *The Sound of Music*, I wasn't Liesl and I wasn't going to play a man's part. I didn't want to become a cheerleader. So I was an athlete. I played softball, basketball, and volleyball. I did photography because the softball coach taught photography. I did what was available. I did some jewelry. I tried band, I played the tuba a little bit, because the marching band needed someone to carry the tuba. I started doing performance art then. I didn't know it. I did off-color acts, like *Saturday Night Live* acts. Instead of Mother Goose, I did Mother Loose. I got in trouble for things like that, but there wasn't a place to put me. The Russian history professor made room. He let me and my friend play in women's drag in an Agatha Christie play. I played a rich lady, and there was freedom in that. Putting on the accoutrements of exaggerated femininity, balloons in my shirt, and exaggerated wealth, giant pearls, and a big hat. I felt free when I wasn't me.

Photographer **J. Cleary Rubinos** made their way from science to art. They remembered:

I stopped being a creative person for a very long time because I thought it was very impractical. I shifted all my attention to being a scientist in high school because I thought that was a very practical route. I went to college for environmental biology and I didn't do anything artistic for a long time. I was only there for about a year and a half and then I left. I became very disenchanted with being a scientist. I couldn't see spending the rest of my life doing that; I would have been a miserable scientist. I remember sitting in the lab one day and we were doing what's known as a western blot genetic test, which is when you take matter from an animal and you pour it out onto gel. It eventually stretches out across the gel, making patterns, and it was a weird revelation watching them form: This was as artistic as I would ever get in this lab. Those tests are gorgeous; there's a lot of beautiful art in science. But I just wasn't happy having that limit. I was like, "That's it, I'm done. This is it, if this is all I can do. I'm out of here." So I left and went to a community college for communications – film, theater, and television. I eventually picked up a camera and now I spend my entire life as an artist. Which is, I think, a lot more fulfilling than spending my days as a scientist.

Taking Both Paths

Sometimes, when an artist comes to a fork in the road, they choose to take both paths. **Tine Kindermann** has successful careers in visual art and music; both passions started at an early age. "I started to sing when I was about fourteen," she said.

My mother would sing to me at home and I took violin lessons, but music was not one of the big focuses in our house. My mother was actually trained as a graphic artist, but she was almost a naïf painter in her style, even though she had studied. She was very much under the shadow of my grandfather, who was the artist in the family. He was a professor of fine arts at the university. My father had this whole Prussian work ethic and it's all about discipline. You're not supposed to enjoy it, but you have to do it. My father had told me that I should make a drawing every day. I unfortunately adapted that and made drawing into a duty for myself. Once I was in Ireland, I didn't want to do them anymore. I stopped drawing altogether. I had a very, very complex relationship with being an artist. I started singing and writing songs when I was sixteen. I taught myself how to play guitar and was very inspired by people like Joan Baez, whom I saw perform in Berlin. I wrote songs and performed them in churches and street festivals. I went to Ireland after high school – that's where I learned my English. In English class, I learned how to dissect Shakespeare, but in Ireland, I learned how to ask how to find the train station. In Ireland, I got a little more encouraged to sing. I sang in pubs, because everybody was singing. You'd walk in and they'd ask, "What song do you know?" So we would sing.

Cecil Castellucci is another multi-domain artist. Their creations, which cover literature, film, and music, share a talent for world-building which they discovered early in life. They remembered:

I played a lot of imaginary games – a lot of paper dolls, Barbie dolls, action figures, Playmobil type of things. I was always telling these vast stories. My mom would be angry with me because I couldn't contain it. I wouldn't just play dollhouse in my dollhouse; it would be out in the world. I would literally construct worlds, whole planets. I would make the living room be Europe and my bedroom would be America. I'd have the dolls fly to each other and hang out in different countries. I was always building huge worlds everywhere and complex, intricate stories among all of these dolls.

These stories show that, even when people's paths seem to include some false steps, the varied experiences often feed into and enrich the art. What may appear to be an irrelevant moment or a mistaken choice may well steer the artist toward a new and unanticipated direction. It leads to a theatrical play set in a wrestling ring, a musical's notably poetic lyrics, or novels with especially acute visual descriptions, historical accuracy, or medical insights. Much as getting lost in a new city may give you fresh insights into the local culture, creative people often draw on all of their experiences, whether directly related or seemingly peripheral, to produce even more complex and sophisticated works.

9 | Eventual Serendipity
All these things just opened up

Whether a young artist has discovered the muse seemingly from birth, after a roundabout path, or inspired by art, at a certain point they are a young adult and ready to start their own artistic journey. However, sometimes they are proceeding down what feels like the right path when there is a slight swerve at the last minute. This little moment of serendipity can nudge someone a little bit or a lot, but either way such moments of fate can have big impacts.

Documentarian **Steven Okazaki** ended up in film by happenstance. "When I applied to San Francisco State University, I planned to pursue painting," he told us.

But the Art department was full up, and the registrar said, "Pick another major, right away, they're filling up fast!" So I grabbed the school catalog, ran my finger down the index and stopped on Film, and thought, "Huh. That's an idea." One, it's creative. Two, I'd learn practical skills – you know, how to run a camera, how to set up lights. And three, you can't make a film alone; you have to work with other people. And, as someone who'd been focused on art and painting since childhood, I worried about making a career of it. Not because I didn't love it, but because I was concerned about my development as a person, mostly working alone and not interacting with people. It's a very insular life. You paint to challenge and satisfy yourself, not others. You show a painting you've toiled over for weeks and someone says, "Hey, that's cool" or, if they don't like it, "That's interesting." It's hard to sustain drive and passion on that quality of feedback. With a movie, the viewer connects or doesn't connect to what they're seeing – they're captivated or bored, excited or distracted – and they're not afraid to say it sucked or it changed their life. It's the people's art form, much more accessible, more honest. So I asked the registrar, "How about Film?" and she said, "Oh, no, Film is completely full, it's the hardest department in the school to get into." That process, dropping art and deciding to pursue film, took about six seconds, shorter than the time it just took me to explain. In six seconds, my life changed.

Muralist **David Guinn** was initially driven to shift his emphasis from painting to murals by a chance sighting combined with an available learning opportunity. "I was living in Missouri in a little farmhouse," he told us.

I had a lot of space and time and was working on oil paintings. I was painting pictures of sculptures by Rodin but incorporating them into my own thing, my own landscapes, so that was the beginning of it ... I moved to New York and I thought it would be exciting to be there and try to be an artist. But that proved to be really hard. I worked a bunch of different jobs. I worked as sort of a freelance artist assistant, did some work for some photoshop design company, and then was a bike messenger. One day, I was watching some guys paint a billboard on Houston Street and I was like, "Wow, that looks really exciting and interesting and fun. I really want to do that." That was a moment. I was thinking I really want to try to paint a mural, do something big. Shortly after that, I ended up moving back to Philadelphia and there was this mural program that was just really getting started. That was exciting because I met someone who was painting murals and he hired me to be his assistant. It was just one of those times. All these things just opened up and started to go well. I thought, "I'll just keep following this path."

For **J. Cleary Rubinos**, a friend's sudden challenge opened up a new door to photography. "I started being a wedding photographer," they said, "because one of my friends was getting married and she needed someone to take pictures. I was not very good at that point; I had just picked up a camera a couple months before. But I wanted to help out a friend." The friend was thrilled with the results. "She told other people who told their friends," said Rubinos. "It snowballed to where everybody wanted me to take their wedding pictures."

Meanwhile, **Tine Kindermann**'s visual art career was jumpstarted by a connection she made while nannying. "After high school, I couldn't decide what to study," she told us.

I was scared of college. I was torn between psychology and art. I forced myself to make a portfolio, and then they didn't accept me. I never tried again. So I never went to art school or college. I took a job as a full-time nanny in Berlin for a costume and set designer. She got me a three-year apprenticeship as a set painter for a theater. That's how I discovered there was a way of doing art that was more hands-on, more like a trade; it had nothing to do with college. The theater thing was great because I was taking things and trying them and throwing them together. It was also really good to know how to learn a craft, a trade, to have something solid that you knew how to do. I would just make these drawings that were tiny; the big thing that I found so annoying about high school was that you had to fill the whole page. I didn't want to fill the whole page. It was very liberating. The funny thing is that when I did actual sets, they were usually flat. They were cardboard and very graphic, and not at all like my dioramas.

Singer **Country Joe McDonald** applied his early knowledge about different types of music in an unusual venue. He remembered:

My father got investigated by the FBI because he and my mother had been a part of the Communist Party in the 1930s. He lost his job at the telephone company before his vested pension kicked in. We went into a downward spiral. A lot of things happened and I started working to help make money for the family at twelve years old. I started incorporating music into my work. It was when I was digging ditches for a trailer court that I heard work songs I'd learned from an Alan Lomax book on songs of North America. I remember trying them out, and they worked really well with the rhythm of a shovel or a pickaxe. They helped pass the day. I sang chain gang songs and work songs that went back 200 years. I also started playing in orchestras on the weekends and in bands for local dances. That was the beginning of picking up extra money as a casual musician – working casuals was what they called them.

Geoff Meed has worked in a variety of roles over a Hollywood career that has spanned five decades, from stuntman to actor to writer to director. Meed's journey began by tagging along with his mom. "I went to the University of Texas at Austin," he said.

I was a little crazy and found myself getting into a lot of trouble. Ultimately, I got kicked out of school and ended up back where I grew up, in El Paso, Texas. I don't know if you've ever been to El Paso; it's an okay place to pass through, but you don't want to live there. When I got home, I was really depressed because my father and brother had both graduated from UT Austin and I had gotten kicked out. I wasn't doing anything. I would go to a class at UT El Paso, go to the gym, and that was it. My mom had always done local theater and commercials. When a film came to town, she'd audition for it. One night, my mom said that the drama department at UT El Paso was doing one of her favorite plays, *The Fantasticks*. She asked me if I wanted to go and I actually really enjoyed it. I met a girl there. I guess between having seen *The Fantasticks*, that girl, and my mother, they roped me into going to the next audition, for *Funny Girl*. I went down and auditioned and got hired for a part. It was something to keep me busy. It paid a little bit, nothing major.

Another movie came to town, *Extreme Prejudice*, and the kids at UT El Paso were going to go audition for it. I asked to go so I could see what was going on. I had no inclination to audition. The casting lady said, "Don't you want to audition?" I said, "No, no, no, I'm just here with my friends." But she said, "You've got a good look; I really think you should audition." So I went ahead and read for a role. Out of all these actors, college kids, and drama students who went down to audition, I was the only one who got a callback. I went back the next day and asked the casting lady, "What exactly is this? Who am I going to read for?" She said, "Well, you're going to read for Walter Hill. He did *The Warriors, 48 Hrs.,* and *Aliens.*" That scared the … poop … out of me. I had no concept of what it was about, so I went in and did terribly. But that made me think: If I'm the only one who got called back out of all these drama students, maybe it's something I should try. I switched my major from psychology to drama. I did a commercial in El Paso and then transferred back to UT Austin and subsequently got cast in everything up there.

Role of Serendipity

For novelist **Gina B. Nahai,** fate walked up to her on the street. "I was in law school at the University of Southern California," she said.

I liked the material that I was studying, but I wasn't sure that I would like the lawyer life. So I was wandering toward my car and I literally happened upon a trailer that was parked on the side of the street. Out of curiosity, I went over and it turned out it was the poet, James Eagan, who had just started a writing program at USC. The program was so new and the school believed in it so not at all that they gave him a trailer. Not even a classroom. He was recruiting people to the program. I said I liked to write, and he convinced me that I should try it. I took a leave of absence from law school and I started taking classes toward a master's degree in the evenings. I started writing the stories that became the *Cry of the Peacock*, about the people I knew and the stories I heard as a child. That was the first time I wrote anything other than an essay.

Fate can open a door, but artists still have to have the insight to recognize worthy opportunities, the talents to take advantage of them, the cojones to walk through the door, and the persistence to keep plugging away. These same abilities can help launch artists toward professional openings even without such a chance occurrence, as we see in the next section.

PART III

Career

10 | Finding Their Niche

I didn't realize there was a place for that

People can start their creative paths in one field and end up finding their perfect fit in a slightly adjacent area. It might take moments or decades to land in the right spot, but the skills and lessons initially learned can still pay off. Even when early careers are not ideal, they can enhance and sharpen the talents needed for these next steps. Exposure, insights, passions, and access to materials can all provide a leg up.

Mark Street enjoyed photography as a teenager, then realized that it was possible to reach the same level of intimacy in film. He remembered:

I still think that my creative roots are wandering around the Midwest, in Wisconsin, taking photographs and searching for something and not knowing what it is. I had this very simple one-to-one relationship between what I saw and what I tried to record. Back then, film was a hermetically sealed world that seemed to be about money and high production values. Then I went to Bard College and saw filmmakers who had that same type of one-to-one relationship with what they saw, a more immediate relationship with the world around them. They tried to make connections between the past and the present. Creativity, to me, is a way to be constantly engaged. What I did as a teenager and what I do now are similar; they're voyeuristic in a way. They're an immediate reflection of things that intrigue me.

Costume designer **Michael Krass** leveraged his way from shopping for buttons to designing for Broadway shows:

I started working at a costume company and I learned everything that way, like a medieval apprenticeship. The company made costumes for Broadway shows, and had a rental business. I was a shopper at first. I went out and I found where the button stores were in Queens, the guy who did welding for the wings to make showgirl costumes, where the best snaps were made – and fabric, of course. I did that for a while. The designers would come in as glamorous people and we were there to facilitate them physicalizing their designs. I became their assistant within the building and I learned a lot that way. I watched fittings with actors. Then people started to say, "Come work for me." I started assisting them and then I would get a little show when somebody would say, "You work at that costume company. Can you borrow stuff?" I'd answer, "Yeah." So I would get hired as a designer to borrow things, to get them free costumes. And now I've been working for years as a designer.

Actor **Doug Jones** assumed his experience in mime and unusual physicality would make him an ideal comic sidekick. Eventually, he realized that combination could open up other possibilities:

When I was in college, I was part of a mime troupe called Mime Over Matter. I hadn't realized all of this nonverbal dialogue had a home on stage. The art of mime really woke up the rest of me; I realized I could really let this flourish. I brought that mime experience with me out to Los Angeles, along with my goofy attitude and this long, lanky body with a small bone structure. I'm 6' 3½", but I only weigh 140 pounds. When I landed in Hollywood, I assumed that I would be taking the sitcom world by storm. I thought that I was going to be the tall, skinny guy who was perfect as a goofy next-door neighbor or a comedic officemate, one of those sidekicks on TV that I watched as a kid. I was sure of it. I didn't realize that these shows were going to die out at some point.

Not being a romantic, handsome leading-man type, I knew that I had to be funny or scary. Those are kind of your options. The funny I understood. The scary, though . . . I didn't realize I had a scary dark side. We all do. You just tap into that; we all have fears of some sort. If you're in the safe environment of a movie set, you can become the monster that creates those fears. You can explore the fun of the dark side, if you can call it that, where it's safe. It turned out my physicality lent itself very well to building creatures upon me or building any kind of makeup on me without making me look too bulky. Some creatures need to be bulky, but I can play the long, lithe ones without looking like a guy in a suit. And that's what the creatures need. I didn't realize there was a place for that.

Tell that to fans of *Hellboy* and *Pan's Labyrinth*.

Samantha Jakus went from cheerleading to singing to finding dance as her home. "My whole childhood, even up to college, I was searching for my identity," she told us.

Like, what does all this mean? What am I doing? What am I trying to say? What am I, what don't people understand about me? How can I know who I am and harness that and do something with it? I was born muscular and I was also raised with three brothers. I was always very physical – running around, climbing ropes. Being strong was always something I identified with – "Oh Sam, she's so strong." Then I started to build up an identity with cheerleading, because I was good at it, and I was known for being "that good cheerleader." My freshman year, I was Sandy in *Grease*. For my senior project, I choreographed a dance and that's when I started to realize that I don't have to have something come out of my mouth. I don't have to project a voice. My body is my new voice. I can get that total feeling just through movement. So that's how I was known: Sam the dancer.

When I was at Temple University, I picked "O Fortuna" by Carl Orff [from *Carmina Burana*] for the first dance I ever made. My teacher said, "You can't use that song because it builds too high and you'll never be able to build your movement that high." So I made this dance that started high, and by the end, I was just like banging my head on the floor. I felt like I could do things with my body that were so intense, like the music, that they would have to accept that I was challenging and matching the music. The dance ended with me just jumping up and banging my head on the ground. It was a little bit painful, but it was okay because I was comfortable going through pain to show that expression at that time. I had three professors at Temple come up to me and pull me into their office and say, "You need to check out Elizabeth Streb. She's doing what you're doing but she's not getting hurt." When I saw her company, I knew I wanted to do it. I remember looking at their video and thinking how brilliant the work was. I thought that if I worked as hard as I possibly can, I could do it. I auditioned. And then I got it. It was like putting a dot in dance history, and I was proud of that.

Circuitous but Inevitable

Mary Roach narrowed down her options to journalism, based on practicality and a blunt assessment of her innate abilities. She remembered:

I became a writer because I graduated with a liberal arts degree in the middle of a recession and I didn't have any job skills. I started out doing copyediting and proofreading, which anybody can do with a little bit of training. I quickly got frustrated with that because it's best left to people who are fairly interested in details and I'm just not anal enough to be a good copyeditor or proofreader. To me, it wasn't creative and, in fact, that did matter. I started writing one day, a couple years after I graduated. I wrote a couple of humor pieces for the "Sunday Punch," which was a section of the *San Francisco Examiner*. Looking back, they were pretty stupid, but they ran them. I realized that having a creative element to what you do for a living made things a lot more satisfying. I moved to doing freelance magazine journalism and a little bit of advertising copywriting. I wrote press releases for the San Francisco Zoo. Writing seemed to be a lot of fun; I was interested in the possibility of being a magazine writer because I liked to travel. Early on, I was happy to be doing any kind of writing because it was better than none. I didn't have a lot of alternatives.

Writer **Cristina García** recognized a passion for literature early in life, but her route to writing fiction had a number of stops along the way. Her education and early career experiences, although in different fields, still provided her with a strong base of knowledge and skills:

I was literally working every spare moment in high school, because my family had a restaurant and required me to help. I continued working in the family business throughout college. It was pretty intense, but that was what was expected; that's what I knew. I didn't like it, but that's the way it was. When I was commuting to college, I took a literature class on the novella. I was a political science major, but it sparked what became a decade of voracious reading for me. The first book we read was Kafka's *The Metamorphosis*. I read it in the Columbia University library and felt this sense of levitation – transported, utterly entranced. From then on, every moment that I wasn't working, I was reading. The class gave me permission to begin reading as avidly as I had as a girl. I was the daughter of Cuban exiles, but I was really an exile within my own family – an exile from myself, from my own proclivities, from my own interests – for a good part of my growing up.

My life was changing, incited by *The Metamorphosis*. But I ended up going, as planned, to graduate school for international relations. I thought I'd become an ambassador. I spoke Spanish, studied German, learned Italian. I was preparing myself for a life in the foreign service. Many of my friends ended up doing just that, or working for multinational corporations, or banks. But when I graduated in 1981, it was the Reagan era and I thought, "How can I represent these policies? Impossible." I knew then that I'd deluded myself, thinking that I could be a diplomat. Instead, I turned toward journalism, beginning as a copygirl for the Washington bureau of *The New York Times*. Journalism is what I did for most of my twenties and into my early thirties. I got to travel, use my languages, covered a wide range of stories. Eventually, I became the Miami Bureau Chief for *Time* magazine. All the while, I was reading, reading, reading. I threw myself into poetry, almost haphazardly, reading Spanish-language poets in bilingual editions. Ideas began marinating until I tentatively began writing myself, poetry initially, which slowly morphed into my first novel, *Dreaming in Cuban*. Mine is a circuitous narrative but inevitable, in retrospect, like all good stories.

Susan Breen also switched from journalism to fiction. "I didn't really write a lot until I got to college and joined the newspaper," she said.

This was during Watergate, so being a journalist was a big thing, very romantic. I think it was one of the braver things I ever did. My first assignment was to write about women's lib. I was nervous to begin with, and I went to talk with a group of women. Everyone had a speculum and was looking inside themselves. I was only sixteen, and there I was with a group of women who were all examining their private parts and oohing and aahing over it. So awkward. My next article was to write about the school replacing their doorknobs. After college, I got a master's in international economics. Not very useful – except it did get me my job as a reporter at *Fortune* magazine. I was a reporter and I did that for a long time.

I can clearly remember the day I started on my first short story. My older sons were taking a nap and *The Godfather* was on TV. I thought to myself, "Do I want to spend the next ten years watching TV?" At that point, I hadn't read many short stories besides the ones assigned in school. But there was a yellow pad of notepaper on the table and I remember picking it up and just picturing this woman who was going to get a haircut. I sketched out the scene and thought, "I can do this." I started off writing simple stories and eventually I sent them out and they began getting published.

Like Breen, children provided a chance for artist **Isabelle Bryer** to redirect her creative energies. "At sixteen, I moved to Lyon to go to a college with an art education option," she said.

We studied art history, painting, sculpture, clay work and nude model drawing. I loved all of it. The art teachers would take us to visit museums and churches as art history education. Later, I took an exam to become an art teacher and failed. I then decided to go to school to learn fashion design and still be doing something creative. I received my diploma and got a job designing evening and wedding dresses in a little shop in Lyon. Being a young designer for a clothing company does not get you a lot of recognition; you are the last person they worry about. The important people in the company are the ones making and selling the clothes; you are just sketching things and having all the fun with seemingly zero effort!

"After about two years in Lyon, I decided I needed to travel. I knew someone who had a fashion trend office in New York, and I offered to do a free project for them to show what skills I had. They hired me as a fashion consultant for very little money. But the job was amazing. They sent me around Europe to sketch and take photos of clothes in trendy stores in Paris, Milan, Barcelona, and other fashion capitals. Then I would fly back to New York where the team and I put together a European trend book to sell to US garment manufacturers. When in New York City, I lived with four room-mates, along with a few mice and roaches, but I felt like I lived at the "center of the world." I was drawing fashion sketches all day long: some loose and artistic ones and some very detailed "flat" technical drawings with neat captions about the garment. I met my future husband in New York, and he and I moved to Los Angeles. I worked freelance as a fashion designer. Interestingly, being French seemed to help a little bit; somehow, people assumed I had an innate fashion sense. When my daughter was a baby, I decided to try painting her portrait. I took an acrylic painting class at a community college. Just that one class put me on the way to finding out what I like to think of as my "true purpose" – if, in fact, there is such a thing.

Sometimes, finding one's niche can be a moment of realizing you have gone deeper and better in your art than you had before. Actor **Maurice Godin** told us,

I remember the first time when it wasn't just learning the lines and doing pretend acting, but actually being in a scene with somebody and realizing that whatever kind of mystery that was going on between us was being transmitted to the audience. The sum was greater than the parts, something greater than either one of us could have done on our own. The first real spark of something authentic on stage was really intoxicating, because it gave me a sense of power – power in communication, power in being fully seen by an audience, and recognizing the connection that comes with that. My whole outlook toward what I did on stage started to change. Instead of the presentational style of acting and the performance I had been doing, I was craving something a little bit more powerful and true.

As we have seen, it can take exploration and self-insight for an artist to find their creative home. But this discovery isn't the end of the journey. Growth continues as artists develop and nurture their skills and abilities.

11 | *Becoming a Professional*
That was where I honed my craft

Once a creator has decided on a particular type of art to pursue, it typically takes about ten years of practice (or ten thousand hours) to become a true expert (Ericsson et al., 2007; Simonton, 2014) – although we should note that this doesn't guarantee that anyone who spends ten thousand hours on a task will become an expert (Harwell & Southwick, 2021). We have probably spent far more than that amount of time walking, but have still been known to trip on flat linoleum. These ten years (or so), however, can follow circuitous or more direct paths.

Writer-producer **Chris Bearde** became a pro under fire. "I was on live television, three days a week for five years," he said. "When you are speaking live, unscripted, for half an hour and getting laughs – you couldn't have a better learning experience. Not only that, I had to light my own shows, I had to write my own scripts, I had to send my own letters out to people. This was the early days of television. That was where I honed my craft."

On the other hand, writer **Charles Salzberg** had to create his own pressure to perform. "I was probably what would be considered a late bloomer," he told us.

I always knew I wanted to write but I didn't do it. Part of it was laziness and part was that I wasn't ready yet. I got a job teaching in a disadvantaged school. It was for emotionally disturbed kids who had behavior problems. The shift that I had was from noon to 4 p.m., so I could write in the morning. That's when I really started to write seriously, because I knew that I didn't want to teach. I liked the kids but I didn't like teaching. I couldn't see myself spending the rest of my life teaching the same subject over and over again. I decided I wanted to get a Master of Fine Arts, that was my plan. So I wrote a novel. A teacher had a friend who was an editor at Macmillan and asked him to take a look at it. The editor said, "This is really good, but what you should do is put this in a drawer and work on your next book." At the time, I thought I didn't want to do that. But later on, I realized that he was right.

It was a good first novel but I had to find my own voice. It did give me the incentive to realize that I probably had a little talent and it kept me writing and I applied to Columbia for an MFA and I got in. I lasted there two weeks. I dropped the program because I thought, "I'm already writing, what do I need this for?"

Resilience and Evolution

Artist and animator **Keith Wong** dodged a number of bumps in the road but kept working until he found success. It started when he made a painting for a friend who had been Miss America. "She hung my painting up," he told us.

One of her friends was a music producer and another guy was a TV and movie producer and they wanted to develop an animated cartoon called *Destructo Man*. They saw my painting and asked her if I was in the business. At the time, I was just doing gallery stuff, trying to figure out what I wanted to do with music, and making this anti-meat pop-up book. They gave me a call and said, "We need someone to come up with some development for a series." I told them, "I can do all that stuff." I grew up wanting to be in animation, so I had taught myself how to do storyboarding and character design. I had never done it professionally, but I told them I had.

They only wanted me to do a couple things, but I ended up doing everything. All the designs, storyboards, and layout. I brought my friends onboard who could do voice-overs. I also composed music for the show. Eventually, they said, "We can't pay you right now, but we'll make you an associate producer." It never went anywhere, but it was exciting to learn. Then, one of the producers was hired to assemble a design crew together to turn a beloved Malaysian comic book into an animated series. He brought me onto the project. There was a full crew, which meant character designers, background designers, and prop designers who would design the objects or vehicles in each episode. There were painters for the backgrounds and storyboard artists. I wanted to learn everything. Eventually, they were firing everybody off and I was taking over all the roles. Pretty soon, the only ones left were me and the painter, and then the painter was fired. I took over for a moment, until I was able to convince them to bring the painter back. I was getting ripped off right and left, but it was a great learning process. Usually, you have to know someone to get into animation, or else you start at the very bottom. That means being an intern, and then a production assistant. You may or may not ever get into an animation position, depending on your tenacity and luck. I got in the door, in a way, without having to do the initial climb. The next show I got was *Rugrats*.

Singer **Country Joe McDonald** had always wanted to become a professional musician but, like Wong, he took a number of different twists and turns:

At seventeen, I enlisted in the navy and went to Japan for two years. I had a guitar, and a friend played the trombone. It was the era of Harry Belafonte calypso, and international music was popular. I learned some Japanese and sang some Japanese folk songs. The international influence of the scales and the sounds of Asian music stuck with me for a long time. I came back and tried to go to college and it was there that I got reconnected with the folk music boom at that particular time. The civil rights movement fit in well with my left-wing labor history and my family. I started to write songs connected with the freedom-song movement to desegregate the South and that sort of thing. There was a folk-song club on campus where I started playing folk music. I saw Joan Baez at the Hollywood Bowl in 1965 and she had a guest, Bob Dylan. I thought, "That's what I want to be, whatever he's doing." That's when I really started writing songs on my own. I dropped out because I just couldn't relate to college anymore. I moved up to San Francisco, not knowing about hippies or anything, and then the whole hippie thing happened. I played acoustic folk songs with other people in coffee houses and they were playing along with the songs that I was writing at that particular time. It turned into Country Joe and the Fish. When Bob Dylan went electric, we went electric and we turned into a rock and roll band. We started playing the music that I was writing at that time, which drew upon all my background from classical to pop to country. Very eclectic. You can hear the Asian influence in the first Country Joe and the Fish albums. I was also interested in John Cage and David Tudor, who wrote classical art music. A guitar player named John Fahey was a big influence on me. He played a steel string guitar and based his stuff on the playing of African American turn-of-the-century blues players and created a whole new genre called American guitar. Our band became very well known for what's called psychedelic rock and roll, and an instrumental piece I wrote, 'Section 43.' That eclecticism, a different kind of mixture of classical and rhythm and blues and country, separated Country Joe and the Fish from what was normally happening. It was unique to that style and was considered West Coast psychedelic. That was what we were doing from 1966 until we played Woodstock in 1969.

Like McDonald, writer **Dara Horn** took a winding route but always knew the final destination:

When I graduated from college it was never, "Should I be a writer?" It was, "How can I find a job that can pay enough to support me and will leave enough time to write?" That was what I was looking for. I wasn't interested in doing anything other than writing. Writing isn't a career choice, it's more like a disease. Seriously, it's as though you found out when you were six that you had diabetes and you had to figure out how to live your life in a way that accommodates the diabetes. It was not a choice of whether I was writing or not; I always was writing. It was more like, "Well, I know I can't be a doctor because I won't have time to write if I'm a doctor." There are a lot of other reasons why I didn't want to be a doctor, too. But the point is that if I went to law school, then I'd have to be a lawyer, and I wouldn't have had time to write. It was any job I was looking at; it was sort of what can I do so I'll have time to write whether during the job or after the job.

I had a couple of ideas. During college I had become very passionate about Hebrew and Yiddish literature, and I wanted to continue my studies in that. I had this idea that if I was in graduate school getting my PhD, I'd have a lot of time to write. This turned out not to be entirely true. But when I was in college, I applied for a lot of jobs. I applied at magazines, I tried to cultivate connections. I also applied for a lot of postgraduate scholarships. I applied for a scholarship that would let me spend one year at Cambridge University in England. The beautiful thing about the scholarship was that you didn't have to do anything. "Here's a lot of money to go to England for a year; here's your room, enjoy." Obviously, it was a very competitive scholarship. They only wanted to give it to someone they thought would make good use of the time and the opportunity. I applied for that and I got it. The problem was I also got engaged. The person I was marrying had a job in the United States for the year after graduation, so if I went to England for a year, he wasn't coming. I was very torn about it. By the time I got the notice of acceptance, I already knew I was getting married. But I decided that I didn't want to spend the rest of my life wondering whether I should have spent the year in England. So I went. I got a master's degree in Hebrew there. But a master's in England isn't like here; it wasn't that hard. I only had to write a 40-page paper. That's not a big deal. It wasn't very demanding and my partner wasn't there, so I was just very lonely and miserable. I sat around for a year being really, really bored. I had that time and space. I'd always been a very motivated student in college. These summer jobs, I was writing for the paper, I was writing plays, I was producing plays, I was always very busy. I never sat around and did nothing. Suddenly in England, I had a year with very minimal commitments and no social life. I had an idea for a novel a few years before but hadn't had time to pursue it. So when I was there, I was like, "Why don't I just try this?" That was when I started writing my first book. It was all because I didn't have anything else to do.

Like Horn, writer **David Morrell** had always wanted to write. He leaned toward an academic path for practical reasons:

In college, I was learning how first-rate books and indeed masterpieces were put together, the approaches that the authors took and the ideas that were in them, and what made one book better than another. I knew that to write adequately, one had to read the best that had been written. I decided that being in an academic environment would give me the structure to read those great books and engage in discussions about them. As things turned out, the way I put my books together was the way I analyzed the books that I taught in my American novel class. I made the decision to get a master's degree because I wanted to learn more. By the time I had my master's, I didn't know if I could earn a living as a writer – I hadn't even started *First Blood* yet – so I said, "All right, I'll get my PhD." I could earn my living studying, so to speak, and get a job as a professor. If I had success as a writer, great, but I had a family to support. I said, "This is a good, dignified way to live, to be with ideas and great works. We'll see what happens."

Actor-writer **Jim Piddock**'s journey was more direct. "I started writing sketches in boarding school," he told us.

We did comedy revues, the usual stuff, doing outrageous impersonations of teachers and getting cheap laughs any which way we could. I studied English literature and language at King's College, London. I spent my whole time there acting and playing soccer but managed to find just enough time to get a degree. It would have been a logical step to go into journalism or something like that, but I knew all the way through that I was going to be an actor. After university, I did a one-year course at drama school, which taught me the technical side of acting. Then I was lucky enough to get a job as soon as I left, doing children's theater, and that got me my British equity card.

Making a Left Turn

Sometimes people take two paths. Writer **Tess Gerritsen** went through them sequentially. "I began writing in earnest when I went on maternity leave," she said.

As a medical doctor, you just don't have much time. But I got to stay home when the kids were small and they were very good at napping. Whenever they went to sleep, I would have a couple of hours and I started working on a book. I was reading a lot of romantic suspense back then and I thought, "Well, this is the genre I want to write in because it's so much fun." My first couple of books were romantic suspense novels. It took me about three books before I finally sold one to Harlequin Intrigue, which is Harlequin's suspense line. It was a romance, one of those paperback romance novels that you could buy in the grocery stores. Even though they were romances, they always had a murder mystery in them. I'm known today as a thriller writer, but the crossover from romance to thrillers was easy for me. It's very fluid, these genres. Romance, suspense, it's all a matter of degree, how much you emphasize the thriller aspect. My first novels were about 50 percent romance, 50 percent thriller. Romance was a great market to break into because I didn't need an agent to sell those novels. After writing nine of them, I found myself veering toward straight suspense stories. That's how I ended up in thrillers. I never went back to being a physician.

In contrast, **Indre Viskontas** pursued both opera and neuroscience at the same time. "I definitely feel that I would be a better singer today if I hadn't gotten the PhD – if I had spent all that energy just in perform-ance," she told us. But her parents encouraged her to have a career outside the arts.

It set me back as a performer. But I'd be a very different singer. I think that a lot of the skills that I gained from my PhD are applicable to the different things that I do. I don't regret it, but when I mentor or give advice to young performers who really want to perform for a living, I don't tell them to go get a PhD. I tell them to go and practice your craft and do as much performing as you possibly can and make that your main focus. My path was just different. I don't feel any animosity toward my parents for having instilled that in me because it's made me who I am, and I am proud of what I've accomplished. But it certainly made it a more difficult road for me as an artist. I had to justify my abilities and when I went back to get my master's in music, I was much older than a lot of the other students. It was a very humbling experience to be in your late twenties and be in a classroom full of these people in their mid-twenties – and not be at the top of the class. It was a great learning experience.

Viskontas also learned lessons from science that helped her in music. Her scientific background helped her draw on the scholarship of Carol Dweck (1986, 2000), who proposed the idea of fixed and growth mindsets. A fixed mindset is when someone believes that they are born with a specific amount of an ability that will not change. In contrast, someone with a growth mindset believes that they can learn, grow, and improve.

I realized that, up until then, I had a fixed mindset, whereas a growth mindset is absolutely critical for the performing arts. I developed a growth mindset through that humbling experience of going back and getting a master's in music after having completed a PhD, so I wouldn't give that up for the world. I had to catch up in a lot of ways as an opera singer, but at the same time, it made me a much more experimental performer than I would have been, because I don't have any fears about what I can or cannot do. I became a specialist in contemporary music, which is often extremely experimental, hard to access, and requires a lot of work.

When Circumstances Change

Other artists know what they want and where they want to go, but have to wait until circumstances allow their success. Actor **Michael Kostroff** remembered,

I was a late bloomer in my career. I was very insecure. I would go in and audition, and I was *not* good at it. I was nervous and shy, and I never worked as an actor in my young years. Now, part of that was because I'm a character type and character types tend to find their careers later; I was always meant to play cab drivers and lawyers and funny uncles. But when I decided to get serious about being an actor and moved back to New York, I waited tables and temped – and never really worked as an actor. At one point, I was reading a postcard advertisement for something in Los Angeles and it listed all the TV shows that were filmed in New York and all the TV shows that were filmed in LA. The difference was so overwhelming that I decided that I would give it another year in New York and if I wasn't working, I'd move. I moved to LA, where several things coincided; I was in my thirties, getting to be the right age for the characters that I play, I was gaining confidence, and I was in LA, where there was a lot more TV work.

In addition to his successful acting career, Kostroff (2019; Kostroff & Garnye, 2022) has also written popular books about auditioning and becoming a successful actor.

Actress **Ann Harada** had a very similar experience. "When I was young, I was a character actress," she told us.

But you can't really get work as a young character woman, you have to wait until you get older to start playing character parts. I was getting some work, people always needed a goofy girl or whatever – but I didn't start getting consistent work until my late thirties. Once I turned forty, it was like, "Ann, where have you been all this time?" Meanwhile, that's when I had my kid and my life was exploding around my head. But it was great, it was very freeing for me to realize that I don't have to be like everybody else. I remember trying so hard to be what they wanted and now I feel, this is it.

This is me and you know me and if you think I can fit into your show, that's awesome, and I can bring something unique to the table. You know what I am and I'm giving it to you and I'm not pretending like I'm somebody else. This is so much more freeing and so much more creative because you're spinning off of yourself. You're not trying to do something you are not. It's okay that I'm not the leading lady. It's okay that I'm not the ingénue. It's even okay if I'm not your pick for the character, because look at all these other actors who are awesome. We're all unique, and as we get older, we kind of accept that and don't fret so much. I remember having a girlfriend, we were both coming up at around the same time. She was also Asian, but she was much more conventionally of the type. She was beautiful and she could dance and she had long legs. I said, "Let's just make a pact right now that we're not going to get all jealous and weird about stuff. You get what you get, and I get what I get, and no hard feelings." And it worked. Once you say it out loud, it's not the elephant in the room. We are what we are and we're going to get what we're going to get.

Sometimes, you build your artistic career brick by brick, only seeing your path in retrospect, when you realize you've become a professional artist. Other times, it is less a realization and more a thunderbolt. Such big breaks, as we see in the next chapter, can be once-in-a-lifetime events that launch a career.

12 | *Making It Big*

Sometimes you just get money ideas

What do you think of when you hear "making it big?" Is it a rock star, mic in hand, singing their popular hit center stage? Is it the filmmaker watching his movie open to a packed and rapturous house? Is it the writer waiting for the bidding war to end before her first bestseller is released? Or, all of the above?

When **Bruce Kimmel** began to shift from acting to filmmaking, he knew he had a surefire idea for a smash. "Sometimes you just get money ideas," Kimmel said.

I was working in a place where you called people and took surveys – it was all a bunch of out-of-work actors. We used to go to what they called nudie movies on 42nd Street and 8th Avenue. They were just faux pornos; there was no porno then. You could find hardcore, but these were nudie cutie movies. People would simulate having sex and they would be naked – the girls but not the boys – and they were so bad they were hilarious. We would just go and scream with laughter. I got the idea that we should make one, but a musical. A nudie musical. I wrote some songs, just as a joke. One was called "Orgasm," another was called "Lesbian, Butch, Dyke." Someone in the group did a little poster. We were going to call it *Come, Come Now*. When I got back to LA, I played the songs for Cindy Williams [Shirley from *Laverne and Shirley*], who was a really good friend of mine. She said, "Oh, we have to do this. We have to shoot it in 8 mm and change our names and wear masks." It just kept coming up because it was such a great idea. Porno had come in. To spoof that industry with a musical was a very funny idea. I remember auditioning it for people. I met a guy who had a similar idea to do a musical nudie. He had done some soft-core porno, and we met and decided to work together. At that point, it was going to be non-SAG [Screen Actors Guild] and Cindy and I were going to change our names. She always wanted to be a part of it. Then I actually wrote the script for what I called *The First Nudie Musical*; *Come, Come Now* became a film within the film.

Somehow, we found the money. We found ten people who put up about $15,000 each. By this time, we were going to shoot in 35 mm and we were SAG, so we could all use our names. I brought a lot of people from Los

Angeles City College who I'd gone to school with onto the project. I wrote it, starred in it, and co-directed it [with Mark Haggard]. We started shooting the film on Cinco de Mayo in 1975. I had never directed a movie, but you learn by doing. Mark would say, "We'll do this shot," and I'd say, "What do you mean, this shot?" I'd look through the viewfinder of the camera and say, "Okay, but what if we come over here – would it be more pleasing?" Then the cameraman said, "You're not going to be looking through the camera all the time." I said, "I think I will be. I'm here to learn. I want to know why you're doing things." And we had a great time. It's not what you would call a great movie, directorially. But it is funny with great performances and that was the only goal. We had an Academy Award-winning editor editing the film, but he didn't really understand the comedy and we ended up letting him go. I ended up going into the cutting room with his assistant and the other leading actor, and we cut the film in twelve weeks. It was my lesson in filmmaking. I would sit there and go, "Can't we cut to this other shot?" I was told, "Yes, if you had shot the other shot, you could cut to it." I would go, "You mean we should have shot that other coverage? Oh, well." I learned to shoot coverage and protect myself. We took it to Pasadena for a full house of strangers. Nobody knew what to expect when they saw the title, *The First Nudie Musical*, and the filthy dirty print that we'd been carting around. There was a disclaimer at the start that they were about to see a work print; it's a work in progress and we're just gauging audience reaction. Within two minutes, they weren't just laughing – they were screaming with laughter. They never stopped for the entire film. I thought the man in front of me was going to die, he was laughing so hard and stomping his feet on the ground. This movie had the kind of language and risqué scenes that had never been done before on film, to this extent, just wall-to-wall nudity. It was pretty outrageous, and it's been ripped off a lot since then, so it doesn't have that kind of shock value today. It was not salacious; that's the joy of the movie and why it's lasted all this time.

Big Break in Slow Motion

Other times, big breaks take a slow path. Visual artist-entrepreneur **Phyllis Brody**'s success with Creativity for Kids was a natural evolution of her passion for arts and crafts. "Creativity was just always a part of my life," she told us.

I grew up in Brooklyn and my mother took me to Pratt Institute on Saturday mornings where I took fashion illustration, drawing, and all kinds of classes for a number of years. When I was at Brooklyn College, I worked at the Henry Street Settlement House overnight camp during the summers. I was a counselor the first year, and then the next three years the arts and crafts counselor. When it came time to graduate, there was a decision point and I had to decide if I was more interested in the arts or the social work side. I didn't think I was good enough to be an artist – I mean, I was measuring myself up against Van Gogh, for example. It never occurred to me that I could go into museum work or graphic illustration. Those career paths were undeveloped in the late 1950s. I didn't want to go into advertising or fashion because it didn't fit with my social values. Plus, Henry Street had a wonderful psychoanalytically oriented counseling program that fascinated me and there was a dawning sense of social justice that I wanted to incorporate into my life. Since I was ready to experience life outside of New York City, I chose to attend the social work master's program at Case Western Reserve University in Cleveland. I met my husband there and we got married between my first and second year of graduate school. I loved putting my creativity to work making curtains and other things for our apartment.

I worked for several years in family and youth counseling not-for-profits and then became a full-time mom. I was home with the kids when they were little and began trying out different arts and crafts. Starting with paper collage, I moved to assemblage and then to different types of dimensional quilts. When I started to exhibit and sell my work, I began to take myself a little bit more seriously in terms of having a little more confidence that I had some ability. When I was selling my work and exhibiting and entering shows, I was successful in the sense that I did sell a lot of work. But I wasn't a production person. I didn't want to be on the traveling art circuit. It was not a way of life that appealed to me. I never saw myself setting up a booth and selling my work. I just never wanted to get into art as a business.

Along the way, I began doing a lot of teaching and workshops in schools and museums. I met the woman who would ultimately become my business partner when we were volunteering in our children's classroom. She had been trained as an artist and also had a law degree and we were both pretty much based at home. Everything was geared around the kids' schedules. Together, we discovered that fantastic transformations happened when we gave the kids simple creative projects. This was very powerful as we saw their raw, natural creativity shine through. We realized that no one had turned these experiences into products, so we decided that we would try. I was already making little kits and sending them to my friends who wanted their kids to be creative but didn't know how to get started. And that's how Creativity for Kids was born.

Eventually, Creativity for Kids became a major player in the field of kids' toys.

Sometimes, a big break that took many years can look like an overnight sensation to the outside world. Writer **Mary Roach** remembers the story of her *New York Times* bestselling debut, *Stiff*:

An editor from *Discover Magazine* called me out of the blue one day and asked me, "Would you like to do some science writing?" They had read some of my pieces in a magazine called *Hippocrates*, which no longer exists. It was a smart health/medical magazine that won a lot of national magazine awards, so other editors would try to hire the writers. I said yes, and it turned out to be fascinating. Even though I didn't have a background in it, they ended up being the most interesting stories I'd done. Then I did a column for *Salon.com* when it was new and very popular. An agent contacted me at about that time and said, "Do you have any ideas for a book-length project?" Which is how they say book. I looked over at my columns and their hit rates, to see how many people had read them. There were two or three columns related to cadaver research that had the highest hit rates of most of my columns. I thought this topic seems to be something that people find fascinating. So I just threw it out there as a possible topic, and the agent liked it and said, "Why don't you write a proposal?" A bidding war started, and that was it. Bear in mind it was fifteen years of magazine writing before I got to the books.

Sometimes, an artist gets the call suggesting they do an exciting project that will become their big break. Other times, it is the artist who makes that call themselves. Writer-producer **Chris Bearde** remembered:

I was trying to get into television and ply my trade as a comic. I'd been doing stand-up comedy at that time – very badly, in little clubs. Then I got a letter back from Steve Allen. I was so surprised. He said, "Look, you want to get into television any way you can. And once you're in, then you can build your way up into something." So I was just looking around for what I could do and I found that there was an audition for a kids' show. I auditioned for it. A strange thing happened: I actually got the part. So I had to do a kids' program. It was during the week and I could do whatever I wanted. They wanted me to read books to kids; it was so inexpensive to do television shows at that time. I would just sit there and read a kids' book in front of a camera, and that was a half-hour show! But I had been doing these poetry routines in jazz clubs around the city. I had a little three-piece jazz band and I would read or speak poetry in between the jazz sets.

When I started to do the kids' show, I thought it would be great to do that on television. I called Theodore Geisel, Dr. Seuss – and he actually picked up the phone. It was amazing. I've got a television show, and now I'm talking to Dr. Seuss. I asked him if I could read his books on television in Australia for free because I didn't have any money. I was fiddling around trying to get something going – and he said sure. So I read Dr. Seuss with a jazz cadence in the background. It was so advanced, but I didn't know that. I would say, "The cat in the hat came back" and the flute would go doo-da-da-doo-doo. It became a very successful little show. All these American comics would come down. They'd be up late performing in the clubs and then they'd sleep until four in the afternoon. They'd be watching my show and they'd be calling me and saying, "It's great, what are you doing there in Australia?" And I'd say, "That's where I live." That was the beginning.

Perseverance Is Key

Singer-songwriter **Julie Gold** also made her luck from humble beginnings:

I wrote "From a Distance," and I pitched and pitched and pitched it. And it was rejected, rejected, rejected. Then Nanci Griffith recorded it. My last year working as a secretary at HBO, I went on the road with her for a week. I played Carnegie Hall with her once; I played piano and she sang and my whole family witnessed it. Her recording of "From a Distance" set the ball in motion, but I still needed to work at HBO. A year later, I left my job in good faith. I cried my eyes out to my parents one night. All my friends were getting married, they were all having income and cars and houses, and I said, "I can't struggle anymore." They asked, "What do you want us to do? We'll do anything. What can we do to make your life easier?" Although my parents were very middle-class, I said, "Can you pay my rent for six months? That's all I need, six months to live like a musician." "Done," my mother said. "Do you want it all at once or do you want it once a month?" I said, "Once a month, so it feels like I'm working." And so I left HBO, and I dedicated that whole six months to doing nothing but writing, pitching, playing. At the very end of those six months, I got my first royalty check from Nanci Griffith's performances. That bought me the next six months. In those next six months, Bette Midler recorded "From a Distance." And I never, ever had to look back. An amazing chain of events. It was exactly the right time, and though I didn't have any success with all of the letters I wrote and all of the stuff I sent, karmically, I believe we can make these things happen.

Other times, an artist might give themselves a set time limit to produce a pièce de résistance, only to have it work in a very indirect manner. Writer **Chang-rae Lee** explained:

When I graduated from college, I was grateful to have gotten a job. I certainly didn't have a writing project in mind. I worked for a year for a Wall Street firm. My roommate at the time was already writing and he had received a book contract for a novel, and that spurred me to think, "Maybe I can do this, too." I thought about a project during that year and, at some point, I felt I was ready to give it a shot. I didn't hate the job at the firm. It was perfectly fine, a real job, and a decent one at that. I thought I could always go back to it if I had to. I had an agreement with my parents about this. I told them, "If it doesn't work out in five or six years, I can easily go back to regular work." So I quit to try to write. Soon after making the decision, my mother was diagnosed with inoperable stomach cancer. It ended up being a good thing, quitting the Wall Street job. It allowed me to spend as much time with her as possible, which I'm sure she wouldn't have been happy about if I was still working for the firm. In many ways, it seemed right to start my writing life while with her. I finished the project, a novel, a short time before she died. Unfortunately, it was not a publishable work. It perhaps showed some promise, but it was not a novel anyone would want to read through to the end.

After my mother died, I decided that I had to put it away for good. I think at the time all I really aimed for was to get a book published – more about affirmation than about making worthy art. Writing that novel was about a certain kind of performance, to show myself and the world how clever I was. But I wasn't really engaging with anything real, and it showed in the final draft. I realized that it failed because I didn't really care that much about the novel itself and all that the story required. And I thought to myself, particularly after my mom died, "I have to start growing up. I can't just play around and pretend to care about things. I should write a story that I care about, or not write it at all." That's when I applied to graduate school in writing and I ended up going to the University of Oregon, for my MFA. And that's where I started *Native Speaker*. The concerns that arose were drawn not exactly from my personal experience but surely from the things I'd thought about for a long time, about identity and assimilation and the role of language in my life. I wrote the story in a different way, too, with a special focus on its way of telling. I suppose I made a kind of artistic commitment to this, along with the usual attention to the narrative and characters, a commitment to my rhetorical mode.

Native Speaker won the PEN/Hemingway award for Best First Novel and was the first novel by a Korean American to be published by a major American publisher.

First Time's a Charm

Every so often, an artist hits the ball out of the park on the first pitch. Playwright **Kristoffer Diaz**'s *The Elaborate Entrance of Chad Deity* was his first produced work – and an Obie winner and Pulitzer Prize finalist. "At NYU's Gallatin School of Individualized Study, they pushed us to find connections between the things that you're interested in that aren't traditional," he said.

So you can take a sociology class, an art history class, and a political science class, and then it's up to you to figure out what the connective tissue is between them and why those are your interests and what you're actually looking for. So that's something that has impacted my art. In the case of *The Elaborate Entrance of Chad Deity*, I took professional wrestling, politics, and race and ethnicity and figured out how those disparate things were all connected – or why they all felt connected in my own head. *Chad Deity* was the first thing I ever had produced. The very first production was in Chicago, and a few months later we came to New York. It played off-Broadway; for my first real New York production to be at that level is rare – let's put it that way. You don't usually start out at that level. I had been working in the theater for seven years doing small developmental workshops or writing plays without them being produced. I had been doing that a bunch, and I guess I had put in enough time in the minor league world to jump up to the big time with the first production.

Writer **David Morrell**'s *First Blood*, in addition to being a bestseller, added an iconic character whose name has entered the lexicon around the world: Rambo. He shared with us how chance and timing can determine what makes it big and what gets forgotten:

Some people can write brilliant books and nobody will publish them and nobody will buy them and nobody will read them because the books don't happen to coincide with what is interesting to the mass population. Other authors might not have the skill, might not be as inventive as others, but have been fortunate enough at a particular moment in a culture to have a topic which at a particular time suddenly was immensely interesting to people. It might not have been interesting the year before, it might not be interesting ten years later, but at that moment, it changes the culture. I wrote *First Blood*, about a Vietnam veteran coming back, hating what had happened to him in the war, and getting into conflict with a police chief who had been a war hero in Korea and didn't understand why Rambo would feel as he does about Vietnam. If that book had been published in 1975, it might not have had an impact because America was getting out of Vietnam. We lost. Nobody wanted to think about Vietnam then. I know how hard it was to write that book. But I also know how easily, if it had been published at a different time, it could have been ignored.

Reading about these success stories is voyeuristic fun. However, being an artist isn't just about fame and acclaim. In the section to come, we'll talk about the realities of being an artist, from its impact on family and friends, to the need to support oneself, to what it means to change one's artistic focus, to grappling with issues of identity and culture.

PART IV

Realities

13 | *Navigating Personal Relationships*
Art is a selfish activity

When most people think about a life in the arts, they might assume it consists of moments of inspiration and struggle, brilliant successes and bleak lows. But for the vast majority, reality lies somewhere between lying drunk in a gutter and touring the world on a private jet. In the real world, living an artist's life can complicate romantic relationships. It can pit the need to make a living against the impulse to follow one's art. In general, there are a number of realities that don't make the pages of the tabloids and glossy magazines.

What does it mean to try to maintain a loving relationship with someone while still staying true to one's art? Artist-animator **Keith Wong** acknowledged the challenges of sharing a life with a creative artist. "My mind just keeps going," he told us.

At times, I'm like this hermit, an art hermit, because my wife and everybody might be saying, "We're going to go camping, we're going to go skydiving," and I'm in my little laboratory. I just like creating. Once I have two things going and I'll have this other idea and I'm thinking, "Oh my goodness, that's really going to be fun to work on."

The financial instability of a life in the arts can also hurt a relationship – and the art itself. Musician **Jim Tobbe** remembered:

In my last year of law school, I realized I absolutely hated it. I was working as a law clerk at a law firm in Cleveland. I was engaged and had to tell her that I didn't want to be an attorney. I had a fiancée who thought she was marrying an attorney and she ended up marrying a jingle writer. She came from a very structured family; her dad was a cabinetmaker and was home at five o'clock for dinner. That was what she wanted in life – structure and stability. Starting out in the jingle-writing business was tough. I remember my oldest was a year and a half old and he had a double ear infection. We were having a terrible time getting him to sleep. We'd just gotten him on medication and he was crying; we put him in bed with us and finally got him to sleep. A musician's clock is a night clock. At one o'clock in the morning, the phone rings about my work. The baby woke up and started screaming and my then-wife yelled, "That's it – you're getting a real job." I tell people that was my last day at the jingle-writing business.

Compromise and Sharing a Life

Despite such challenges, there are success stories, such as that of writer **Tess Gerritsen**. "I must give a lot of credit to my husband," she told us.

He was willing to put up with a woman who not only had a medical job but had this all-encompassing hobby that would sometimes keep her up late at night. He was unhappy with that because it's a hobby that takes you emotionally away from people around you. Writing is dealing with people who don't exist; it is being wrapped up in life that doesn't really exist. The real people around us can't always stand that. It was always, "Are you listening to me? Where are you? Oh, you're away with your characters again." Having a spouse who resents your writing will kill your career. A writer once advised: "If your wife doesn't like your writing and you are, at heart, a writer, get rid of your wife. If you are really a writer, you can't proceed with a marriage like that, when something that is so much a part of you is not allowed to flourish." I'm sure there have been divorces over this issue. Eventually, my husband came to understand that this is a part of me; it's something that you can't extract from me. And now that I'm successful, he's delighted because it allowed him to retire early.

Painter **Shanee Epstein** also found she had to choose between spending time on her art and with her family.

Art is a selfish activity, and I've had a very hard time doing things for me or for my art, as opposed to anybody else. It's challenging saying "I can't help you today; it's my painting day." That feels like a selfish thing. So that's a struggle. Self-imposed, completely self-imposed. If my husband came home from work and the house was completely a mess and there was no dinner and I said, "I spent the whole day painting," he'd say, "Oh, that's great. Let's see what you did." But when I realize I haven't painted in two months, I feel the imbalance. The times in my life that I'm healthiest and most productive are when I'm balancing everything, which includes painting. I do better as a wife, as a mother, as an educator, and as a community member when I myself am balanced.

Writer **Dara Horn** shares the world of her art with her husband in an unusual way. "I'm thinking about my characters all the time," she said.

I'm always thinking about them, like they're people I know. My husband has a normal job and comes home at the end of the day, and at dinner, he talks about people he worked with during his day. I talk about people I worked with during my day. Only his people are real and my people are imaginary. These are my colleagues. The only thing is you can't fire them ... We guess about other people's behavior all the time. The only thing I've done that's different is that it is no longer connected to an actual person.

Artist-musician **Tine Kindermann** has also struggled with balancing the often conflicting demands and needs of art and family. But unlike many others we spoke to, she has found inspiration from the resulting exhaustion:

People sometimes think of artists as parasites who do things for their own pleasure. I have struggled with that notion because I think of my father's Prussian extreme self-discipline, where if something gave you pleasure, it wasn't to be pursued. I have learned to allow myself to do what I'm doing. I have to take the time to make things. That's selfish, especially when you have kids. When I had a little baby, I was thinking about my experience of motherhood. I took this icon of motherhood, the Virgin Mary, and I painted Madonnas who were tired and had bags under their eyes and they were carrying pots. Because I felt like it was so destructive, how women are supposed to behave as mothers.

Motherhood changed artist **Lex Marie**'s art dramatically as well. "Prior to motherhood, I used to paint and draw things that I saw," she told us.

I could see a landscape and I could paint it how it looked. But for some reason, once I had a kid, I felt like painting and drawing and telling my own story. So I began painting myself. I began painting my child and painting things that we encountered. Then, once I did that, it became so much more personal to me – and because other people could see that it was personal to me, they ended up relating to it as a mother or sister or daughter. I started telling stories. I felt the need to capture specific moments. One painting was called "Potty Time," and it's abstract, of me sitting on the toilet, with my son sitting on his little potty next to me. These super-specific moments where I'm trying to relax, but I have the baby monitor by me, they actually happened, but I think that other parents could relate to it. I've never seen that in art.

Art Opening Doors

Just as some artists can find inspiration from their personal relationships, at other times personal relationships can benefit from their art. "My mother was a very good storyteller," writer **Susan Breen** told us.

I think had she lived now, she would have been a writer. She had Parkinson's and when she went to a nursing home, it was very difficult. At the same time, I got this job [at the Gotham Writers Workshop], which was only a couple of days a week. I saw her pretty faithfully at least once a week, usually twice a week. When I saw her, I would give her my lectures – I would talk about point of view or something. It was sort of silly, because she would raise her hand and say, "I have a question." Then we would discuss. It brought us together. She would tell me stories about her life that I hadn't known. This went on for a number of years and then she died quite suddenly. I had been writing fiction for some time, short stories. I had tried writing two other novels, but they were not published. So I thought, I want to write something about a family, a mother and daughter whose fiction brings them together. They heal their relationship because of writing fiction. So that's what led me to write *The Fiction Class*.

However, other artists, such as singer **Country Joe McDonald**, have found that a good family life can come at a price. "The more happy I am in my personal life – with my family and feeling comfortable with myself – the less creative output I have."

How People Treat You

Being an artist can not only complicate romantic relationships but can also affect how people perceive and treat you, for better or worse. Sometimes people feel curious or excited. Other times, they may become jealous or annoyed. Actress **Donna Lynne Champlin**'s early talents caused resentment. "I was kind of an explosion of artistic creativity," she told us.

I was a dancer, a pianist, an actress, a singer, a writer, a flute player, a visual artist, etc. I think if I'd been good at just one or two things, it wouldn't have been so bad. But because I was good at a lot of things, and winning a variety of competitions, I always seemed to have a lot of people mad at me – frustrated teachers who wanted me to make their subject my main priority, jealous kids and sometimes, even worse, their parents.

People may respond negatively to artists because they unconsciously see the lack of creativity in their own lives. Novelist **Diana Abu-Jaber** beautifully articulated this:

I think that we all need some sort of creative outlet. It is necessary to understand ourselves. We find different ways of managing that need. A lot of us suppress it because I don't think our culture really supports it. I don't think we really recognize creativity. If anything, I think people look at creativity as kind of kooky. I think that creativity is a need and that people can actually get angry, sometimes, when they see other people pursuing their imagination and their creativity. I think it threatens a lot of people because they see the loss in themselves. Often it makes people emotional, upset, angry, sad, and defensive when they don't have it themselves.

Indeed, several studies have found that people can have a bias against creators, even if they may not say so or even fully realize it (Katz et al., 2022; Lee et al., 2017; Mueller et al., 2012).

Occasionally, an artist may think that they have found a community, yet end up being the only one to stay the course. As writer **Cecil Castellucci** related:

I thought when I was growing up, all those people I went to high school and college with were all on board to be artists. I thought we were making an agreement that this is what we were all going to do. But twenty years later, not many of those people are doing art. They've put away those childish things and become serious.

Of course, there can advantages to the public's perception of artists as being different. Actress **Ann Harada** admitted to us, "I like the way I get a little leeway from the rest of the world. People see me as a little artsy. It's like I get a little pass."

Sometimes, people are simply intrigued by artists and want to know more. Actor **Doug Jones** shared:

I find that people who live in the left-brain, ducks-in-a-row organized world, treat you differently if you're an artistic, creative person. If I'm at a public function or a party and what I do for a living comes up in general conversation, I find that someone who comes from a "Yes, I'm an accounts receivable manager at blah-blah-blah corporation" will be absolutely fascinated when I say, "I'm an actor." I've found that people treat you differently when they realize you're *not* an accounts receivable person at corporation X. It's a whole world that's fascinating to them. There are fewer career opportunities in the creative arts, fewer jobs in those fields than there are in the corporate world. There are fewer of us out there, so when we are spotted in public, it's more of a fascination, "Oh wow, what makes that person do what they do?" So I don't open my mouth and start talking about myself in public forums unless I'm ready to tell the whole story.

However, the exact reverse can also be true, as photographer **J. Cleary Rubinos** related to us: "There are some people who don't sing in the shower, don't write, don't paint, don't take photographs, don't knit – they don't do any creative stuff at all. I've met those people and I think they're a little weird ... A little boring."

Being Creative but Not in Charge

It can be a challenge to be creative when you do not have the final say about how your work is distributed, marketed, or approved. **Bruce Kimmel,** the actor-writer-record producer, struggled with a studio head playing dirty three weeks into the run of his directorial debut, *The First Nudie Musical*:

As I later found out, the head of Paramount Distribution called Ted Mann of Mann Theaters and asked him personally, as a favor, to pull the picture. I had a friend working for Mann Theaters, and he called me right after and recounted that conversation. That was all I needed. I did something that killed my career for a few years – I went public. It was very stupid of me. Because they don't care, they only see somebody causing trouble. Even though we were right to do it. A 28-year-old upstart can't take on Paramount Pictures. So that was bad. We ended up getting the movie back from Paramount and we got a small distributor in New York who loved the film. They opened it a year later in New York, where it ran for three months straight in one theater. It was a huge hit. The week it went wide into more theaters, we were the fourth-highest grossing picture in the nation. It was very embarrassing to Paramount. I didn't work at Paramount again for many years and I was blacklisted at ABC for a few years.

Not all people in power are like that, of course. Some have real insights into what makes an artistic work a success. Writer **Lisa See** remembered:

When I finished *Shanghai Girls*, I had ideas for the next book and I went back to New York to meet with my editor. We were talking about three of my ideas and working out the holes when the publisher walked in and said, "We want you to write all of those books one of these days, but first you've got to write a sequel to *Shanghai Girls*." I really resisted the idea because to me the end was a new beginning, which I liked. But I'm nothing if not an obedient Chinese daughter. So I went home and started doing the research. By the time *Shanghai Girls* came out, I had finished all the research for the sequel, *Dreams of Joy*. My first book event was in Philadelphia, and the first question was from a woman who'd read an advanced copy. She asked, "Are you going to write the sequel?" And that turned out to be the first or second

question at every book event, from every interviewer, from every book club –
all the way until one week after *Dreams of Joy* came out.

Indeed, *Dreams of Joy* made its debut at #1 on the *New York Times*
bestseller list.

If human relationships are one driving force in life, money is
another. Balancing the pursuit of art with earning a living can be its
own challenge – as we will see in the next chapter.

14 | *Making Money*
How are you going to eat your creative writing degree?

The idea of the struggling creative doesn't come out of nowhere (although the real-life connection is not terribly strong; Acar et al., 2023). Often, pursuing your creative dreams is not the most secure way to earn a living. For every Stephen King or Taylor Swift who can afford a small island, there are thousands who are just trying to keep their electricity on. The stereotype of the starving artist should not be taken literally. Novelist **Diana Abu-Jaber** summed it up neatly: "If, God forbid, you tell somebody that you want to be a writer when you grow up, they look at you with pity. How are you going to eat your creative writing degree?"

Some artists are lucky enough to have a family that helps. Writer **Dana Sachs** told us:

I had financial and emotional support from my family to try to do the things that I wanted to do. If I didn't have that, it would have been a much, much bigger deal and bigger risk to decide I was going to try a creative field. There are not a lot of ways to make money as an artist or writer. There are plenty of people who try, but they are very expensive careers. Writing is less expensive than filmmaking, but there are many concrete costs. I can talk all I want about psychological risks and being willing to think about my own creativity. But unless you have some kind of support from your family, or some other kind of support, it's a lot harder.

Writer **Tess Gerritsen** was able to pursue her art while she raised her kids and her husband brought in a salary. "I always knew I wanted to write, but I needed the ability to feed myself in the meantime," she said.

Most writers don't make a living for quite a while; it takes a couple of years, if ever. Becoming a writer is a big risk. You take creative risks as well. I was lucky to be in a spot where I could stay home. Because I also had kids to raise, I didn't have to justify why I was staying home, plus I also had a working spouse.

Two Artists = Twice the Challenge

When two artists end up together, it can become even more complicated. Writer **Peggy Orenstein**, married to filmmaker Steven Okazaki, described the balancing act:

For me, the creative life is not divorced from economic reality. I make a living as a writer, which is something I'm very proud of and grateful for, but it also influences what I can write. My income is not secondary to my family; I'm married to somebody who does a similar kind of work. Both of us have done very well, but even so, we're still an independent journalist and a documentary filmmaker trying to build a life in the Bay Area. So that creates some pressure. I have to consider the marketplace and that, to an extent, shapes my ideas. That's not all bad, it forces a kind of focus, but at the same time, it can't dictate everything, that would be soulless. If I try to only think, "My editors and my audience are going to like this," well, I can't do that or even, honestly, predict it. My work ultimately has to be driven by my own curiosity and desire. As an example, when I was right out of college, I had the idea that maybe I would write romance novels, those formulaic Harlequin books, because it seemed easy and like a fast way to make a buck and I was making so little money, barely scraping by. But I couldn't do it, because I don't read those books and I don't care about them. So, while it's a balance, in the end I have to write what engages me.

There are many ways that artists can make enough money with their art to support themselves. For example, singer-songwriter **Julie Gold** had a little bit of luck to go along with her talent – in the form of a smash hit song:

I continue to compose, but if it weren't for "From a Distance," I'd still have to have a day job. I had a publishing deal for ten years during the greatest success of "From a Distance," so I was a paid songwriter for ten years. I am surprised that out of everything I've written, "From a Distance" is the only one that the general public knows. I wish that that wasn't the case. I am grateful for "From a Distance," and I know it changed my life and continues to.

People's eyes light up when I say I wrote "From a Distance." They ask, "Really, really, what else?" I'll say, "Well, unless you lived in New York or you're a Patti LuPone fan or a Patti LaBelle fan, just very fringy stuff." Which I'm proud of, but there's nothing else that's a bell ringer. I really think "Good Night, New York" is my best song – it's a beautiful song. I fished in a humble pond. Daily, though. I loved fishing in my humble pond and I took great pride in my humble boat and my little fishing rod and my bait. And I believed. I fished in my humble pond daily and God granted me a whale. All I did was reel it in.

Alternative Sources of Income

If artists don't have a big hit that brings in royalties for years, they need to be able to find other sources of income. Ideally, those can come through their art. For example, musician **Jacob Hyman** told us, "We were in commercials for Starbucks, Chevy, and Target, and that boosted us. These things are a steady income – especially when they use the part of the song with our voices. You get Screen Actors Guild royalties, which are really high. There's all these little ways to get money."

Sometimes, art is financially remunerative – until it's not. Musician **Jim Tobbe** was making a successful living writing jingles until technology changed the situation. "We used live instruments; my partner could play pretty much anything," he said.

The problem was that, by the early 1990s, computer technology started getting good enough that a kid in New York could produce music that sounded just as good as ours for a couple hundred bucks. But ours, with live musicians and everything, cost thousands of dollars. It was so hard to say our stuff would sell better because it was live. What I tell people is that we made enough for one of us to make a great living, but not enough for two of us. I'd still be doing jingle writing today if there was any money in it.

It can help to be savvy about how to market oneself. Opera singer-neuroscientist **Indre Viskontas** explained,

Branding is extremely important in the arts, especially when there are so many things that compete for your attention. The business side of being an artist is more important than it ever was before because there are so many people out there. It's so easy to get information, so you have to funnel people to the right part of you that you want them to remember. You need your elevator speech: "This is who I am, this is what I do."

Musician-theater artist **Steve Riffkin** also recognized the importance of earning a living. "I went to good schools and absorbed a certain amount of knowledge in the fields that were of interest to me," he said.

But the degree was never important because I knew it would never matter in what I wanted to do for a living. People weren't going to hire me because I had a degree in any of these fields. They would only hire me because I was actually good at what I did. Nobody hires anybody in the arts because they have degrees – nobody. It doesn't matter. You only get work in the arts because you have something of value that people want to pay money for. Practicality plays a huge role; you have to know how to make your art pay. In certain cases, 90 percent of your motivation will be money. God knows, I did a Christmas princess ball for daddies and their daughters. The fathers showed up and immediately ran to the bar and got drunk and let their little girls in their little pink dresses run around for the next three hours eating as much sugar as possible; what they did not ingest, they threw at each other. That was the most horrible gig – but I was well paid. Although there are some gigs that are *not* worth doing again – like that ball – no matter how much money they're offering!

Earning money from art can mean more than paying the bills. For artist **Isabelle Bryer**, money was a marker of reaching a certain level of accomplishment. "It took a long time to finally decide I could call myself an artist," she told us.

It finally felt real when I started consistently selling my art. Once in a while, I would sell a large piece for a lot of money. If someone in my family called, I might mention that I had just sold a piece for $3,000. I guess it was to say that I was contributing financially to my family with my art, because I knew "artist" didn't sound like a real job to them.

There are those artists, however, who see their work only as a way to make money. Although writer **David Morrell** has had tremendous financial success from creating the character of Rambo, he holds disdain for such artists who create with the sole purpose of monetary gain. "I disagree with writers who use focus groups," he said.

They ask, "What kind of book would you like to read? What kind of characters do you like? What if I did this other book?" It's as if they're at a mall, ticking off slots on a public-opinion form. True creativity – expressing oneself to make something out of nothing, to create something that wasn't there before and is distinctive – that requires a different attitude. I tell my students to write a conversation with themselves, explaining why they feel compelled to write a particular book, why they're the only people in the world who could have written that book. I encourage them to be first-rate versions of themselves and not second-rate versions of other authors. The only thing we have that matters is our time, so why spend it asking other people what we should do?

Scraping By

However, many artists – unlike those Morrell mentioned – find it hard to market and sell their work. As muralist **David Guinn** told us,

Figuring out the balance of the making-a-living part is difficult because there isn't a career path with specific milestones or anything like that. My father had specifically decided that he was never going to try to make money from art because he felt that it would compromise it. I tried to support myself by doing screen-printed t-shirts and also hand-painted t-shirts. I was interested in the idea of it being a career. But it turned out that I hated doing the selling. I didn't know how to do it. I didn't have any model for that. It's been hard to feel comfortable with not making a lot of money. The financial unpredict-ability has been one of the hardest parts of this life. The fear, perhaps completely irrational, of judgment has driven me to work very hard, putting in lots of time beyond what the financial compensation warranted. I've let art – a mural, a show – take precedence over my physical and emotional health. I think more structure and predictability would be good, would be healthy. I wonder whether what I'm doing is the right thing to do.

Phyllis Brody struggled with similar issues with her personal art. However, she was able to launch a very successful business, Creativity for Kids. "I never had a problem selling the Creativity for Kids products as I did selling my own art," she said. "Because one was *me* that I was selling and the other was a product that we had created. It was much easier for me to be more commercial with our business, to promote it and to try to convince people about it."

Beyond selling your work, there is also the issue of needing to raise money to do your art in the first place. Lyricist-librettist **Bill Russell** told us,

Doing theater is very expensive, even to do a reading of a musical. With a play, if you cast it well, you can pretty much do a cold reading and have a sense of what you've got. But with a musical, they have to learn the music, even if they're holding it in their hands. You have to hire actors for a week and you have to hire musicians – at least a pianist – and rent space in New York City, where real estate is so expensive. But it can be a dangerous thing because if you do it too early, [potential investors] can get turned off if you really haven't worked on it. You only get one shot with some people; they won't come back if they don't like what they see the first time. It's a tricky equation sometimes. That's why they call it show business and that's a whole aspect you have to consider. Money is a big issue with theater.

The degree to which art requires financial investment can vary by domains. Filmmaker **Greg DeLiso** said:

If you are a folk singer, you can just take up your guitar and put a song down and you're done. If you're a painter, you just need to buy some paints. But for a filmmaker, even to do some simple thing, there's thousands of dollars of equipment to buy and all kinds of people you're dependent on, like people to act in your movies. It's a big logistical thing.

Such responsibilities are particularly onerous for independent artists. Filmmaker **Steven Okazaki** recounted: "The feature documentaries I've made cost between a half million to a million bucks. If you're an independent filmmaker, in order to do the creative work, you have to do all the other work first – the grant writing, the meetings, the pitching, the unending hustle for funding. If your funding doesn't come from a single source, everything is a struggle."

Day Jobs

Sometimes, despite having talent and drive, art is not enough to live well or even fully pay the bills. Painter **Shanee Epstein** shared, "I've never had the freedom to do my art full time because of financial reasons. I don't see creativity as something that stays on paper. I don't see my life as an artist as something that I only do in the studio on Monday and Wednesday."

Photographer **J. Cleary Rubinos** agreed, telling us:

An artist's kids are going to know that they won't be able to have the material possessions that their peers can have. It's just not going to happen, and you have to be okay with that. I think that's something that every full-time artist has to be okay with. I don't have awesome clothes, I don't have awesome shoes. But I'm okay with my secondhand shoes and my clearance-rack clothes.

Even when art does not bring financial rewards, many artists find it is rewarding enough to be worth the struggle. For example, photographer **Greg Friedler** told us:

Making a living as an artist is a brutal, brutal thing. I hit up against it every day and it sucks. Point blank, it sucks. And the deal is, I tried to do the commercial thing but it never worked. My photography is way too raw for the American market. I got enough work to get by. But they would always be like, "No, dude, this is art, this belongs in a photography gallery." Sometimes, I go to the photography galleries with my "Naked" stuff [a book series with artistic photographs of average people clothed and unclothed] and they say, "Wow, this is incredible, this is out there, but I can't sell it to my collectors." So it's been super-duper challenging because it's been an extreme amount of rejection. I always tell my students that if you're not getting rejected constantly, you're doing something wrong. You have to get your work out there and the only way to do that is to present it to people who won't always get it or like it or promote it or show it.

One of my favorite sayings is that art is a lifelong calling which will supremely challenge one's will, stamina, and fear of rejection. That's an artist's existence wrapped into one sentence. The art world is a brutal world and I think that people who have a way to make a living and then produce their art are probably more balanced than people who are scattered and trying to sell art in different places while working little odd jobs. I think that, in the end, it's helped me that my art hasn't been taken on by the galleries and the museums. If I found a gallery that sold my photographs and they were selling like hotcakes, it would be a blessing and a curse. Their clientele would want to see more and more and more. That's why there are a lot of artists in New York City who are huge, huge artists but they don't ever do different things because they get pigeonholed. That's what their collector base and the world wants to see. So they just keep doing the same thing over and over again. For me, change is everything. I like being able to wake up one morning and do something completely different that afternoon. I live for that.

Although lyricist-librettist **Michael Colby**'s musicals have won awards and played off-Broadway, they do not bring enough income to allow him to focus solely on his art. "I have created a lot of plays and I've had quite a communal theater experience," he told us.

I've never gained world fame or been able to make a substantial living at it. But there's been a great deal of satisfaction at having my theater families for these different shows. I see other people attain the success I would like to. I would like very much if one of my shows had been successful enough to maintain my being able to make a living in the theater. I teach – I'm a substitute teacher – and I have had shows that have made some money but not substantial enough for me to feel I can do this full time. I'm not self-sustaining from writing musical theater. I think most people in musical theater will say the same thing. I've had great personal triumphs and professional triumphs but not financial anchors. I have plenty of compensation in other regards and I have a wonderful family. While I wouldn't be teaching if theater were self-sustaining, I do enjoy it and I have kids who think of me as the Pied Piper. On balance, I'm very happy with the way things are.

Unfortunately, having day jobs as an alternative way to support yourself while you create your art can be a necessity. Novelist **Gina B. Nahai** encourages young writers to make sure they have another way to support themselves:

I think the pressure of putting all the stakes on a writing career, from taking on a mortgage to giving you a sense of accomplishment, is just too much pressure on a writer. You need to be sure this is what you're going to do and that you can make a living out of it – or at least have a strong enough sense of self to not question your story if a publisher rejects it. It takes a while. I think it's always good to have another job. I was a consultant at the RAND Corporation for three years while I was writing *Cry of the Peacock*. After that, I had a day job in the manufacturing district downtown, then I taught writing at the University of Southern California for nineteen years.

Musician **Peter Litvin** may win the prize for the most interesting, albeit temporary, day job. "I started out trying to record artists and make money, but nothing was working out well for me," he told us.

I got distraught and said, "Forget this. I'm going to go get a day job and focus on making music that I like." I was devoting all my time to trying to get some artist to record who I wasn't even into. I ultimately wound up not having the time to record the music that I wanted to record and make new songs. In the midst of searching for a job and not finding one at all, I thought of ways I could make money recording music. I wore an alien costume and played guitar on the streets. The music had the kind of groove that people could bob their heads to and dance, and some people have come up and rapped when I played. I did it all over – in Bay Ridge, Union Square, Park Slope, Times Square; all over the place. I definitely did not have a strong desire to go play funk music on a guitar in an alien costume on the subway. But it was fun to do and it made money. If I could go down there for a couple of hours and make $50, I'd rather do that than get up at 6 a.m. and get on the subway to go to an office and not make a whole lot more than that after taxes in eight hours. It was producing a pretty good amount of money, but all of a sudden I got a summons to go to court one day when I was playing in Times Square. So I quit doing it altogether.

When all is said and done, the relationship between art and money remains unpredictable. As singer-songwriter **Country Joe McDonald** said:

When I get a feeling out in a song and communicate it to myself, I feel successful. But it doesn't always translate into financial success. And you can also have a song that's a hit with the audience but is not financially success-ful. I know it sounds paradoxical, but it's true. In other words, they like the song, they sing the song – but they don't buy the song.

15 | *Different Creative Areas*
Don't want to box myself in

If you're creative in one way, does it mean you have an edge in other types of creativity? In other words, would a creative novelist be more likely to be creative in another, distinct area, such as solving mathematical equations or cooking? Or does creativity in disparate areas require such different abilities or knowledge bases that this same novelist would not have any particular advantage when trying to paint a portrait? That's a recurring debate in the academic study of creativity, which is often called domain specificity versus generality (Baer, 2022; Chen et al., 2020; Qian et al., 2019). If creativity is domain-specific, then our novelist would be no more likely to be creative in painting – or designing blueprints for a building, keeping a small child entertained, or doing home repairs without all the necessary supplies. If creativity is domain-general, our novelist should have at least a small edge at being creative in sports, animal training, or computer programming. Scholars have largely converged in the middle, with the idea that creativity has some parts that are specific to a particular field and others that are more general to any field (Baer & Kaufman, 2005, 2017). Artists, however, have their own wide array of insights and opinions.

Artists draw distinctions between domains – even between closely related ones. "There's some enduring quality to fiction that nonfiction doesn't have," writer **Gina B. Nahai** told us. "*Cry of the Peacock* came out in 1991, and people are still reading it. A few years after that, because of that book, they started the Iranian Jewish Oral History Project. They published multiple volumes, but nobody is sitting around reading those books. They have them in their homes, but they don't read them."

Similarly, writer **Dana Sachs,** who writes both fiction and nonfiction as well as doing translations from Vietnamese, said:

When I think about nonfiction writing, I think about molding your life into something that makes sense as a story. Our lives don't always have the dramatic arc that a story has. Fiction is sort of the other way around. Fiction is creating everything from nothing and you can go in any direction at all … I also love translations. I think it's the most exciting of the literary endeavors I've ever done. I think of myself as finding a beautiful sculpture that Michelangelo made, but it's covered in mud. You're not making the sculpture, but you're cleaning it. You're making it available to other people. You have to think of a way to honor the writer's ideas in a different language, using different words. If you can't think of the right word, you have to keep thinking about it until you come up with what makes sense. There's a beautiful epic Vietnamese poem with a certain rhythm to it, like Shakespeare's iambic pentameter. Do you try to create a rhythm in English that mirrors that, or do you try to focus on the meaning? You can't do everything. If you see the writer is doing something with a certain kind of sound, maybe you can evoke a similar feeling. It's not going to be perfect, but you try to reflect the intention of the author as much as you can.

Balancing Two Careers

Different areas can vary in the ways they reward the artist. **Indre Viskontas** pursues music both as an artist and a scientist. She has conducted empirical studies on music (Slayton et al., 2019; 2020) and written academic books on the topic (Viskontas, 2019). At the same time, she has performed and directed numerous operas:

I enjoy the feeling I get when a scientific article is published, but the day-to-day monotony of the scientific work is not as pleasurable to me as the day-to-day monotony of singing. I realized that I could probably leave a bigger or more expansive legacy as an academic, because I published fairly quickly, but my day-to-day life would not be as satisfying if I weren't able to spend that time doing things that were a little bit more creative. It's a balance between what you spend your days doing and what is going to be your mark on the world. People for whom those two are in sync are very lucky and they're often very successful. But when those two are out of sync, as they were for me, it's more of a challenge. But at the same time, I feel that it opens the door for things that are much more innovative.

As we can see, some fields offer benefits that are longer-term, such as legacy, whereas others give the artist more short-term rewards. Singer-artist **Tine Kindermann** told us,

Singing is much more immediate. Showing my diorama boxes is much safer than being on stage. The boxes are one step removed from me. If someone resents them, they don't resent me physically. Whereas if it's my voice, it's me. But on the other hand, the rewards with singing are much more immediate. I mean, you work away on something for a long time and then three months later you present it in a show but you're already onto something else. It's very satisfying to have your work acknowledged, but when you sing, you establish contact with your audience immediately. The audience is actually a part of what you're creating.

It is not only the benefits that vary from one domain to another. The creative process itself can be different, even when two areas are strongly related.

Actor-composer-artist **Gordon Goodman** agrees – and adds that these differences can impact his process:

There are some creative domains that are more immediate than others. Music is immediate. One musical phrase can prompt the next phrase and then the next. I'll get ideas based on what I just played, but if I forget one phrase, I might forget the other. I find thoughts are like that, too. Previous thoughts build to the next thought, but I have to write it down or new thoughts cover up the old ones. Painting and drawing aren't immediate like that – although I might sketch something immediately. Sculpting's definitely not immediate. Writing is also a lot less immediate, at least for me. I don't just start writing a book or script; I have to have a basic skeleton of beginning, middle, and end before I know what the characters want, and certainly before I can give them any dialogue.

Often artists use different skills to succeed in separate artistic areas, even if these areas are closely related. "When I'm on stage, I'm pushing the energy out, I'm pushing the story out, I'm delivering it to the viewer," actor **Michael Kostroff** said.

When I'm on TV, I'm inviting them to come watch; I'm staying where I am and allowing and inviting them to come over and figure out what I'm doing. If you are too aggressive in your acting on television, it reads as false. It just seems strange. On stage, it's necessary because people are not looking at a close-up of your face; they're not seeing the nuances. The camera can see you think. I had to learn this when doing drama on television. I don't have to demonstrate; I don't have to do anything more than thinking and feeling. I think and feel and the camera sees it. And sometimes, it's the scenes you're not even in that provide context for what your character is thinking or feeling or doing. I'll give you a perfect example. In one scene, I played a lawyer in court who was lying. Normally on stage, you'd have some little awkwardness or perhaps something that would help the audience know that you're lying. But in this particular episode, it was the scene before and the scene after that told them that I was lying. They didn't need me to do anything except be very good at lying. I played it like I was telling the absolute truth and I didn't have to do anything to it. It was context that told that part of the story. With theater, there's certainly room for subtlety, absolutely. It doesn't require histrionics and kabuki-style gestures, but the ideas and the emotions need a little push, a little tap to get out into the room. I once noted on stage that I was adjusting because I was in a theater where the balcony was farther away. I needed to give the ball a little more of a tap to make sure that everybody in the last row got it.

Making a Switch

When Kostroff switched from acting to writing, that was a bigger adjustment:

Now, writing, like many of the best things in my life, came to me by accident. I seem to fall backwards into things and I like it that way. I was working at Disneyland doing a show that involved improvisation and the head writer said, "You should be writing for us," and I said, "I'm not a writer." He said, "It doesn't matter – you should be writing for us anyway." I thought, "Well, I'm sure this won't go very well, but I'll give it a shot." They went wild for everything I wrote. I didn't know I had that ability. I didn't go to college and I haven't been trained as a writer in any way; I'm not even much of a reader. I just love words. Every time I got hired to write, I always felt like it was Take Your Kid to Work Day and I was putting on a suit and pretending. Now I'm a published author and I write a column and I take great joy from that. I like that I get to correct it, hone it, polish it, and make it better. It's like having an unlimited number of takes. And I like when I have a deadline and I think I'll never make it, then something happens in the home stretch and, magically, I get inspired and deliver good work in the nick of time.

When novelist **Lisa See** experimented with different types of writing, she found new ways of expressing herself. "I started out as an art history major," she told us.

Art has always been a significant part of my life. With *On Gold Mountain,* I got to express myself in three different ways: writing the book, writing the libretto for the opera, and curating a museum exhibition based on the book. With opera, you're telling the story through the pure emotion of music. With an exhibition, you have didactic text, but mostly you're telling a story in a purely visual way. I learned a lot, and I think there's a very big difference between the books that I wrote before I did those projects and the ones after. I took those ideas of telling a story in a purely visual way and telling a story through pure emotion to write with new focus. The first book after that was *Snowflower and the Secret Fan*. That was very different from my previous three novels, which were mysteries. *Snowflower and the Secret Fan* is a mystery without a dead body; it's a mystery of what's the secret hidden in the fan. The structure comes from mysteries, but the way I told the story – being more emotional and visual – comes from those other projects.

Writer-actor **Jim Piddock** sees his two creative outlets as completely separate. "Writing and acting are my two main things," he said.

I don't write great stuff for myself though! Writing and acting are two very different sides of my brain that don't work in tandem. In writing, you consider the big picture, whereas acting is much more specific and singular. It's very much about what you're doing; you don't care so much about the whole package. I suppose, if you put a gun to my head and said, "You can either act or you can write, you have to choose," I'd pick acting. It's much, much easier. You basically just have to show up. Although acting in theater is a lot harder, and I did a lot of that in the early part of my career. There are people who love the theater and grudgingly do film and television. I'm not one of those actors. I love the process of film and television. I love the pace of it. And, as I get older, I like it even more.

For **Cecil Castellucci**, the story is the thing, no matter the format. "The goal, the thing that I've always wanted to do since I was a little girl, was just to tell stories," they said.

The interesting thing to me about young adult novels or children's books is that that's when I fell in love with reading, through children's books and young adult novels. With young adults, everything is happening to them for the first time, so it's a real fertile time for them as characters. It's their first love, the first time they've been betrayed, the first time they've driven a car. My first book was a young adult novel; that's how the story wanted to be told. But my first screenplay had adults in it. Although I like a lot of things that fifteen-year-old boys like, like my Xbox and comic books and science fiction, I'm also a woman. I have questions and stories about that which I want to tell, too.

Telling stories in different ways is helpful for me because I can satisfy all the kinds of questions that I have in different forms. I feel like there's an unconscious question that I'm asking, and the answer is what the story becomes. What I find now is that I'm telling stories in different ways. I just don't say no to the way that a story presents itself to me. Rather than thinking I'm just a novelist and so I can only write novels, I just let the story be what it wants to be. Visual artists say, "I'm going to bring my sketch book and do some pencil sketches," or, "now I'm going to do it in India ink," or, "now I'm going to do it in watercolor." They just pick up a different pencil. For me, all of these forms of telling stories are just picking up a different sort of pencil, in a way. A different tool. I write novels, I write young adult novels, I write picture books for little kids, I write short stories for adults and children – science fiction, regular adult stories. I used to be in an indie band, so I wrote punk rock songs. I was commissioned to write a libretto for a company in Montreal, so I write operas. I write plays, I write films, I make short films and long films. I do performance art pieces, I've done stand-up comedy, which is sort of telling stories in stand-up comedy clubs. If I haven't done it yet, I'm going to try to do it eventually, I think. The story announces what it wants to be. My agent sometimes asks me, "Can't you write that idea as a book first and then maybe make it into something else?" And I say, "No. I can't. It has to be what it wants to be." If I can get someone to fall in love with stories, then I've done my job.

Visual artist **Lex Marie** also focuses on the similarities across different ways of being creative. "I certainly don't want to box myself in and just be a painter or just a sculptor," she told us.

The common thread throughout my work is childhood and motherhood, so I ground myself in that. I love learning and taking classes. I learned welding. I learned a lot of different mediums, and they're all things that I put in my toolbox until I feel like I need to pull one out in order to best execute a piece. I see combining my sculptures and textiles with painting at some point, because I just love painting. I don't see myself locking into or settling on one medium per se, even though I think that is often safer or more accepted in the art world.

Many people have an arts bias, associating creativity specifically with the arts (Kapoor et al., 2024; Patston et al., 2018). Even within the arts, there are sometimes perceived differences in prestige; poetry, for example, is sometimes seen as a purer form of art than some others (e.g., Penny, 2008). However, filmmaker **Mark Street** argues that it's easy to see artificial differences across artistic pursuits.

I think it's a completely romantic notion to have a hierarchy of sanity or strange taxonomy of what is more precious to us. I don't really get it. Are poets more precious and journalists more prosaic? Everybody's insane and so is the creative process, if you let it enter you. Wasn't Hunter Thompson crazy? It makes zero sense to me; why shouldn't journalists be as neurotic as everybody else? I don't understand the distinction. I think there's room for madness in all realms. I think that should be as strong in journalists as in poets, prose writers, or visual artists.

For actor-composer-artist Gordon Goodman, it all revolves around creativity:

I always feel that creativity is creativity no matter the domain. Some people are creative in one area and not in others. I just never had the fear that I couldn't create what I wanted in any domain. When I choose a model – I don't think, "Should I paint her or make a statue of her?" That's already decided in my mind. There's always that voice telling me I might not be able to complete it, but if I listened to that voice, I wouldn't do anything.

Career Switches

Switching from one type of writing to another type of writing is one way of changing domains. But sometimes, artists shift to different types of creative works that are not as closely related. **Bruce Kimmel** has gone from acting to directing to record producing to writing novels and memoirs. He told us how one transition happened:

In the 1980s, everything changed for this whole group of actors that had worked all throughout the 1970s. The casting directors changed. They suddenly got power and it was this whole other world. It was just awful and I just stopped working. I don't know why. I was thirty, and it was painful. You'll hear that same story from a lot of actors who came up in the 1970s. You started having to read for casting directors, and I found that offensive. I ceased going out on interviews. So I had to redirect. It was financially very hard. I wrote a lot of scripts and plays, not all of them got done. But creatively it was a very good time for me; that was what was interesting about it. In the late 1970s, acquaintances of mine started a label called Varese Sarabande and it was going to fail. They asked me to invest in it. For $2,500, I could have owned a third of it. But I didn't see it being successful. I said to them they should do soundtracks because there is no niche soundtrack label. I think you could do well, and your first soundtrack could be *The First Nudie Musical*. Their first soundtrack LP was, in fact, *The First Nudie Musical*, and over the years, I helped them get projects. Within five years, they were the biggest soundtrack label. In the mid 1980s, they signed a distribution deal with Universal; I would have been a millionaire. I got so upset when they signed that deal that I started a label. It was an amazing company called Bay Cities, and we did close to one hundred releases in three years. But it was very small potatoes and we had a small distribution system. We did have a huge following and we were getting new soundtracks and had reissued a lot of Broadway shows. I was chomping at the bit to become a real record producer, instead of doing reissues of other people's work.

Kimmel has since founded two additional labels and produced more than 180 original albums, receiving two Grammy nominations.

Dancer-psychologist **Paula Thomson** traded in an artistic field for a more academic one. "When I gave up my dance company and decided to retire as a dancer, I began training as a clinical psychologist," she told us.

This opened new avenues of exploration, including research. I began researching because I wanted to find evidence to support my belief – which I still hold close to my heart – that performing artists are amazing people. In fact, I am married to an amazing performing artist (actor, director, writer), I teach performing artists, research about performing artists and creativity, and clinically treat performing artists.

Thomson's husband, **Maurice Godin**, has been making a similar transition. "I found that acting jobs are like a muscle," he said, "so I started taking classes after my last series was canceled. Things like human interaction and line memorization, those real basic aspects of acting, they get rusty unless you exercise them. So I would go to class in order to spark my imagination and keep the brain well-greased in between shows." Godin found he really enjoyed being in the classroom.

As the shows became fewer and farther between, the class and the work I did in class became more interesting than the work I was doing in my professional world. It's great to get paid well, but it's not a lot of fun when you show up on a set and you're a suit. In fact, I did a series called *Suits* and played another lawyer in a suit. I started working with my wife at the university and I found that exhilarating – working with the young people, coaching them on acting.

He began directing students and then even progressed from straight theater to other areas. "I ended up directing a couple of chamber operas there and I do that every year. I love working with people who are beginning their creative experience in the world and encouraging that first spark of creativity on stage where they realize the efficacy and the wonder of what you can create between yourself and the audience."

Pursuing many different creative pathways may have its risks, but they can be vastly outweighed by the rewards. Opera singer-neuroscientist **Indre Viskontas** said:

I'm sure there are people who would criticize me and say, "You're never going to master any of these things because you have too many pots on the stove," but it's in my nature. Anyone who's ever known me since I was a kid has known that this is the only path I could take. It's just who I am. It doesn't necessarily mean I'll be the best opera singer or the best TV host or the best academic. But maybe I'll be the best opera singer-neuroscientist, and maybe there's something important about that. The idea of becoming a Renaissance person and developing multiple talents and multiple skills is becoming less frowned upon and more accepted. Maybe my path is to forge a way and demonstrate that you can lead a fulfilling and successful career without being constrained by what society thinks should be a particular straight and narrow path.

And, perhaps, that is at least part of what the creative life is all about.

16 | *The Artistic Identity*
A leap of faith

For many (if not most) artists, their work is a key part of who they are. Their creative efforts help shape their identity and how they see themselves in the world. It is not just the generic notion of "being an artist," but rather their specific field, style, and project that define their self-concept. Indeed, some scholars have noted the parallels between creating art and creating an identity; both involve generating different possible ideas and ultimately choosing the best one (Barbot, 2018; Kaufman, 2023). Yet when people try on a new identity – whether by changing how they dress, speak, or act – they typically only help themselves. When an artist explores who they are with words, images, movement, or sounds, it benefits all of us.

For novelist **Chang-rae Lee**, writing is an integral part of how he looks back on each day. "I write about certain things because that's what's possible for me," he said.

I'm just limited, being like everyone else and subject to my time and place in the cosmos and the prevailing culture. Over the years, I've been asked many times why I write, so at some point you have to think about the question seriously. So why is it that I write? Is it for money? For fame? For adulation? All those things can be nice, but ultimately, I wouldn't enjoy the money or recognition if the work didn't compel me – if I were, say, simply going through the motions, even if those motions ended up being "successful" or effective. I suppose I'm always thinking about the next project. Otherwise, I'd feel a little useless. And then if I'm not writing or not writing well or things aren't coming together, I can actually begin feeling sick physically. There are a lot of those kinds of days. I don't expect myself to have to write all this great stuff, but as long as I write a couple good sentences, a good paragraph, that can salvage the day. My mood depends a lot on putting in a good day's work and getting something decent out of it.

Art is also a driving force in lyricist-librettist **Bill Russell's** life. "I have to create," he said.

If I go for a month or two without writing, it becomes a need for me – I have to do it. Although I will burn out a bit after a big project. Sometimes I won't feel like doing anything for a while but then it comes back. When a show closes, the feeling can be postpartum; I often have depression after a big project ends. Getting the show on takes an immense amount of concentration and focus and so all of that is pulling toward that opening night. When that's over, it's like the bottom has fallen out of my life: What do I do now? My whole being has been so consumed with that great experience. And when it's over, there is a feeling of – what's next? And gee, I loved that ... I just have this need to write.

Calling Yourself an Artist

As novelist **Diana Abu-Jabar** was taught early on, though, wanting to make art is different from wanting the label of artist. "In a creative writing workshop," she said, "the professor asked us to make sure that we were more in love with writing than we were in love with the idea of being writers. And that stuck with me – the idea that there was an identity to writing, that being a writer was a valid way of being. That hadn't really occurred to me quite so explicitly before."

Novelist **Gina B. Nahai** also wrestled with calling herself a writer, in part because of her background. "I lived in Iran until I was thirteen years old and then I went to boarding school in Switzerland," she said.

I moved to the United States when I was sixteen to go to college. But at the time we left, there was no possibility in my mind or in anybody's mind that one could be a writer. In other parts of the world, there are certain things that people do and certain things they don't do. The only writers and poets I'd ever heard of all had tragic lives. I didn't know anyone who was a writer or a poet. It was just not at all on my radar or anybody's radar that I knew. English was my third language. I came here two years before the Iranian Revolution. Everyone else started arriving in the United States afterward and they still had the old sensibilities. For years and years, even after *Cry of the Peacock* came out, I wouldn't tell any Iranians that I was writing or that I had a book or any of that, because it was so strange and odd to them. For an Iranian woman, having a profession was not anything people thought about – certainly not something like becoming a writer. It had never been a possibility for me. Then my husband, who was also Iranian but had lived in England since he was little, encouraged me: "You have stories to tell, and you can tell them in a way that makes sense. And that makes you a writer."

Living up to the image of an artist can be difficult at first. "I think I got much more self-conscious about writing in high school and college," novelist **Susan Choi** told us.

I became more aware of writers and writing and, as a result, more inhibited. As a teenager and as a college student I was reading a lot of high-minded literature – some of it really great, some of it not so great. I was sort of in a fog of consciousness about writing. There was a period in my teenage years and even my college years where I was writing much less. Because I think I'd developed much more complicated ideas about what it meant to be a writer and got all hung up.

Similarly, writer **Susan Breen** struggled with accepting her identity as an artist. "The first course I ever took was at the 92nd Street Y," she said.

You had to apply to take their classes and I kept getting rejected. Right after my youngest son was born, I got accepted into the class. I was leaking milk and everybody else was about twenty-four. It took a lot of courage to get up the nerve to go to those classes. People think whatever they can do is something very simple and they tend to downplay it. I see that now in my students: "When can I say I'm a writer?"

Another step is embracing the specific kind of artist you are. Singer-songwriter **Julie Gold** told us:

The desire to create is a very organic thing, you know. I've never wanted to create a painting, I've never wanted to create a moment in terms of a party, I've never wanted to create a meal. I've obviously never wanted to create a child. There's a little bit more, you know, thought that goes into that. I'm not trying to put that in a position of less. But I've wanted to create music. I call them pop songs – they are what they are. I create pop songs. I love pop songs, I love the pop culture, for the average Joe. They're not songs written by, you know, Shakespeare, they're just songs written by the average Joe, hopefully for everyman.

Not only does an artist have to accept their own niche, but so do the powers that be. Actress **Donna Lynne Champlin** knew that her versatility was a plus, but it took time and perseverance to win over others. "You'd think that my versatility would make me more appealing to casting directors, but it just confused them for years," she told us.

It's easier for casting people to label you and say, "She does A, so I'll put her in the A file." But when you're like me and you do A, B, C, D, and E, you don't get put in *any* file because what's the point when another actor does A (and only A) really well? Unless a casting director is looking to save money with a multi-role understudy that had to be able to do roles A, B, C, D, and Z, they'd never call me in. In my first ten years in New York, I only got auditions through friends and people I'd already worked with. But things got a lot better once I stopped working as an audition accompanist – again, it was super-confusing for casting directors: "Is she an actress or a pianist?" – and started working as an audition reader. My versatility came in handy reading multiple characters with auditioning actors all day and I created great relationships with casting directors from behind the table instead of from in front of it. Gradually, they gave me my own audition slots and I started to book roles.

In hindsight, the upside of not fitting into a type has allowed me to avoid being pigeon-holed. I've done plays, musicals, TV, film, voice-overs, played instruments and vastly different characters, etc., whereas my more "type-able" comrades have been limited to doing the same thing over and over. The cherry on this sundae is that I recently found out a casting director who was teaching an audition class actually used me as an example of an established "type." Insane, right? By being un-typeable and refusing to quit for decades, I somehow became a new actor type. Refusing to quit for decades is the new trailblazing apparently. Who knew?

On the other side of the continuum, an artistic identity can encompass a wider array of possibilities. Actor-composer-artist **Gordon Goodman** remembered,

When I was twenty-three, my wife died and I had two little kids. A friend of mine took me to see *A Chorus Line*. He was an astrologer. He had done my chart and he told me, "You may not ever be the wealthiest guy, but you're going to be one of the most interesting guys around." I had no set career at the time and I had no real direction. Often when you don't have a direction, you don't have an identity. We'll do a lot to gain an identity; maybe subconsciously I chose "interesting" as my identity.

What Are You Not?

For an artist to figure out what they are, they must also determine what they are not. After writer **Charles Salzberg** aced the law boards, he assumed he should be a lawyer. But then he started school. "I knew I was going to quit law school on the first day," he said.

The dean got up and he said, "You've read your last book, you've seen your last movie, and watched your last television program." I said to myself, "I don't want a life like that. This is what I like to do." But I stayed a year because I got a deferment from the army. I wouldn't have been a good lawyer for the simple reason that lawyers can't have a lot of empathy for the other side. Lawyers have to be very focused on their side, that they're right and everybody else is wrong. I didn't have that ability – or disability. I couldn't have defended a side that I didn't believe in. I always saw both sides of the argument. As a writer, that's how you get to understand character. I started my first real novel when I was in law school, probably out of boredom. I needed something to do.

Although actor-writer **Jim Piddock** realized early on that he would need his career to involve creativity, he told us:

I don't see myself as being any different, just because I work in a less conventional profession. There are analytical people, there are scientific people, there are financial people. My life just happens to be in the world of entertainment. Although I do tend to want to be creative, whatever I'm doing. If I'm running a soccer team, it's going to be done creatively. If I'm remodeling a house, it's not going to be done by the numbers. Whatever I do, there's almost always some element of creativity involved because I get bored quite easily if there isn't. When I was a student, I tried certain jobs just to pay bills. I worked in an office filing stuff and I was ready to go insane after less than a week. Completely insane, I couldn't stand it. That's why I went into the arts. I couldn't face doing a job that wasn't creative on some level.

Running away and joining the circus may be a childhood fantasy for many, but when dancer **Samantha Jakus** went to circus camp, she realized it wasn't for her:

The program paid you, because you would teach everything they taught you to younger students. That was an old dream. After a couple of months, I realized that it was not where my heart was. To me, circus was just about the tricks, and I'm not really just about the tricks; I'm more about the process that it takes to get to the trick. I like showing that, the struggle and exhaustion, to the audience. At the STREB Extreme Action Company, we would constantly make new work. That's where my passion is – creating new stuff. It's important to me, to be a part of that.

Everyone Is Creative

Another part of artistic identity is the appreciation that everyone has their own original perspective and way of making art. Novelist **T. Coraghessan Boyle** told us:

The great thing about art is that only an individual can make it. I'm not talking about a group, like a rock and roll band; of course, they're all collaborating. But my kind of art. Whether it's good or bad or anybody cares, at least it is solely from the point of view of one individual out of the seven billion alive and the many billion that preceded us. No one could do exactly what I do. Not exactly. Because no one is exactly who I am.

In a similar vein, costume designer **Michael Krass** related:

In creative work, every day is a new question. Every single day you have to be curious, every single day you have a problem to solve – you have to be smarter than anything. Everybody has a different vision of the world, a different set of emotional experiences. Individuality is necessary for creativity. My students are so worried that they don't have anything that's original. But they are original, they can't help it. Isn't your Hamlet going to be different from hers? So, do your Hamlet, for Chrissake, and work your ass off to do it. You have it, you are a creator. Now, do some work.

What does it mean if everyone has the capacity for originality? Academics argue that everyone has the potential to be creative, at least at some level (Beghetto & Kaufman, 2007; Kaufman & Beghetto, 2009). But what do artists think? Actress **Ann Harada** told us, "Who's to say what's creative or not about your life? I think it's creative when I make a new dish or write a really good Facebook status. Creativity is how we operate in the universe. There's creativity that's job-related and there's creativity that's life. I feel like everybody is creative in a different way."

Artist-musician **Tine Kindermann** agrees: "I think that every person is creative. You can make a phone doodle and you're being creative. It's not solving anything; it's just completely useless and fun. I like the word 'useless.' Because there's total freedom in that. Things that are useless are great."

Kindermann adds that creativity expands beyond art. "You can be an artist and not create," she said.

That doesn't take away from your being an artist. Some of my favorite artists have had twenty-five-year creative blocks. That doesn't make them not an artist. How you see the world is what makes you an artist. People always say that certain things aren't art, that they're commonplace and don't mean anything. But, for instance, my husband is a great cook and he's a great arranger of music. To me, those two things absolutely come from the same place. He takes the ingredients and puts them together.

The idea that creativity can be manifested in areas beyond the arts is a common refrain among artists (Baer & Kaufman, 2017; Kaufman & Baer, 2002). Filmmaker **Greg DeLiso** told us:

I think there are different kinds of creativity. If a doctor is doing surgery and something happens and they have to come up with solutions on the spot, you could say they're being creative in a functional way, because there's nothing artistic about that. They're doing it because they have to save this person's life. But at the same time, they're creative because they have to come up with new ideas quickly. Creativity isn't just an artistic word.

Playwright **John Patrick Bray** agreed, saying:

Creativity can be so much more than art. My friend Paul at the bagel shop that I used to work at could make an amazing cold pork sandwich. To me, that pork sandwich was art. I've never had a sandwich like that before. There are some great furniture makers out there who simply carve wood and make a bed from scratch and say "voilà, a bed." There's something really creative about that. It might be the way a person wears their hat, it might be at a jaunty angle, and, oh, that's a creative way to wear a hat. I think art needs to be a little bit demystified.

"To live creatively is to take a leap of faith," filmmaker **Mark Street** told us,

as though it were some sort of religious or spiritual thing. I know people who live their lives creatively who are not artists. There are creative business people and others who are creative thinkers who are not artists, so I don't put it in those terms. I think there are people who make decisions and live their lives as artists without creating anything, in the sense of Andy Warhol or Marcel Duchamp. They make decisions that are very unexpected, just like that's their art. They live to the fullest and I admire that. I think it's a different kind of paradigm.

Writer **Dara Horn** adds:

I don't think you have to be an official artist to be creative. I know people who are creative in their friendships, like when they're throwing a party. My sister threw a party for her husband when he turned fifty. She didn't just throw a party; she made it a *Mad Man*-themed party and people had to come in 1960s outfits. She served things like tuna sandwiches with the crusts cut off, things with bleu cheese. Hard drinks for men. That kind of creation is not limited to people who are in a band or publishing books. People do things with their children, like making up stories. When I would pick up my daughter from daycare, we'd make up a story and every day when she got into the car, we would have a new chapter of the story. You're helping yourself and the people around you to see things in a way they wouldn't have thought to see it.

By contrast, singer-songwriter Julie Gold shared:

I don't think that everybody is creative. No, I don't think so. Or they don't allow themselves to be. Because you have to be unrepressed to be creative. You have to be willing to try things to be creative. Brave and unrepressed. You've got to be able to express things in your cooking and in your painting and in your music. And some people are afraid. You've got to be honest, too. Very honest.

Some Last Thoughts on Creativity

We asked most of the artists about their views and beliefs about creativity. Here are some of our favorites. Novelist Diana Abu-Jaber posed the question:

Is creativity something of the mind or of the emotional being or even spiritual or physical? There are so many layers to what creativity can do inside of a person, kind of unlock different potentials within a person. I guess I think of creativity as a kind of unlocking device. It's something that opens windows inside the mind. And it's suggestive – it's something that tends to ask questions and suggest things without ever being completely prescriptive. It's all about looking at things in shadows or looking at things sideways rather than looking at things directly. Creativity is the thing that invites all that in. It's a kind of wonderful, chaotic energy, the energy of the universe, if you will. For me, I think of it as having a sticky brain. When I'm really feeling creative, my brain feels sticky. I feel like things come through the air to me and stick to me. I don't go looking for them; they come to me. I think that's how creativity works. That there's something about ourselves that opens up and invites things in. You are open to all these different kinds of possibilities and you're letting yourself, you're giving yourself permission to look at things in new ways.

For playwright **Kristoffer Diaz**, creativity involves forward momentum:

I don't know if it's a solution or progress, but creativity means working toward something. There's something about that need to not sit back and settle for what you know or for what's just in front of you but drives you to go a little bit deeper. When you're a kid and you don't understand anything about how the world works, you start to pick things up and play with them. Your first instinct is to put it in your mouth and taste it. And then at a certain point, you start to pick it up and bang it against something – does it make a sound? If it does make a sound, what kind of sound does it make? What kind of rhythms can you create? I think you start telling stories and you start figuring out ways to organize the chaos that's in front of you.

Writer-musician **Cecil Castellucci** offered a wonderfully romantic notion:

I would describe creativity as falling in love with the universe and dreaming of everything being possible. I think that creativity is something that needs to be practiced. It has to be encouraged. It's like a little spark and it has to be fanned in order to flame. Creativity is like a vein that runs inside of everyone. It's always there and everyone has some form of creativity. They might be creative with numbers or engines, but I think everyone has creativity inside of them and it's just a matter of calling it out. The great thing is you can be creative whenever you want, at any age. There's no expiration date on being a creative person. If I'm seventy and I want to be a seventy-year-old ballet dancer, then I can do it because age doesn't matter. There's a difference between creativity and professional expertise. Those are two different things. Being a creative person doesn't necessarily mean that you have to become a superstar.

Creativity can be a beautiful thing, as we have heard. Yet artistic identity includes not only the glorious, but also the mundane. Even the storied life of a musician on the road doesn't match up to reality, as musician **Jacob Hyman** of the Freelance Whales shared:

The fantasy of the artist's lifestyle is just that. It's a job and it's a career and there's sacrifice and there's time away and part of it really sucks – just like any other job. The give and take for an artist is more extreme than the give and take for the normal, everyday working person. Your highs and lows are so high and so low. You can be so high on stage and then you get back and you're in bed with your snoring lead singer and you feel so low. You've been in seven cities in six days and you want to go home but you have thirty-five more days left of touring. You just want to see your girlfriend and sleep in your own bed. My fiancée moved in with me on an October 31, and I left on November 6 for our first tour. She and I only had a week together in our new apartment.

I think it's hard for a lot of artists to maintain a middle ground of emotion and feel okay all the time. Nobody feels like that all the time. There's all this pressure and the expectations of the fans, having to always meet them. Your family and friends saw you play in front of 3,500 people the other night and they expect you to act like a rock star. I think people don't understand what it's like to experience highs and lows like that – and they don't have to. The people who I talk to outside of music expect it to be one thing and I almost feel bad explaining to them that it's not. But I feel even worse playing along. Sometimes I come off as really cynical and ungrateful. But the fantasy when I'm on tour is that I'm making money, meeting lots of girls, doing lots of drugs, and having a great time. But that's just not what a musician's life is like. You're staying in shitty hotels, eating shitty food, you have a limited number of free drinks. You're probably drinking too much. There aren't girls throwing themselves at you – and even if there were, you'd feel too guilty to do anything about it. Either because you're single and you're doing something with a fan and that's weird or because you have a girlfriend at home. I know dozens of musicians at this point, and I only know one who fulfills the expectations of a rock star. When I thought I was going to go on the road, I thought it was going to be all fun – I'd sleep all the time and just dick around and play music and all that. It turns out I spend nine hours a day in a van because America's a huge country and we can't afford a bus. We also can't afford a tech, so I'm lifting all my own gear, loading it and setting it up every night and then breaking it down and putting it in the van. My fantasy has changed. Now I just want a tour bus.

17 The Role of Culture
So many rich untold stories

Just as art can be a source of identity, so can culture (as well as nationality, religion, race, and personal background). Culture can be an artistic inspiration, which can encompass many dimensions. Artists can want to share and teach, to process controversial social issues, and to engage in self-discovery. As novelist **Diana Abu-Jaber** told us, "I feel like my writing, in part, is me looking at the questions that I have about life and trying to understand things better, trying to understand different kinds of challenges and making sense of things. I'm always working things out whenever I write stories. It's about me asking the questions that I want to know more about."

"I think that moving around so much dislocated my sense of home," added Abu-Jaber, who spent her early years going back and forth between the United States and Jordan. "We were always being told that we belonged in another country, that we had another identity. I would say that one of my big themes is the hunt for identity and the search for home. Trying to figure out where we belong and the people who kind of make up our tribe. That's definitely an obsession of mine."

Writer **Cristina García** was driven to explore how immigration can lead to the intersection of cultures. "Sometimes ideas begin with an image or a question or an investigation," she said.

What is it about China and Cuba? I used to go to Chinese-Cuban restaurants when I was a kid but I was never sure how that happened. It was a childhood curiosity – how are all these Chinese waiters speaking Spanish? Or it can be family incidents or secondhand stories. Like *The Lady Matador's Hotel* came from a trip I took to Guatemala with my sister to adopt her eight-year-old daughter. It was something about this hotel we were staying at, something about adopting from another country. All those issues of identity and displacement and the case of Guatemala because that's the country I had in mind when I was writing. It was about the displacement and dislocation that result from years of war – in Guatemala's case, from twenty years of civil war. I'm interested in people and characters who are in transition, whose sense of self is in transition. Identity is mutable in general, but I'm interested in chronicling those transitions. Certainly, my own life has contributed to my curiosity. Immigration has as much to do with transitions as with reinvention. And I'm very interested in that process. This notion of bonding. Where do I belong? What does home mean?

Confronting Hard Topics through Art

For visual artist-musician **Tine Kindermann,** her art can be a way to tackle controversial and even traumatic cultural issues. "There's always a narrative in my artwork," she told us.

I started dealing with most of my German issues when I left Germany. You know, when you see something from far away, you see the whole picture; when you're living right there, you only see the details. I found myself asking why I never asked my grandparents about their life in the Third Reich. I make figures based on the Hummel figurines which came out of Nazi Germany. They are little innocent children mimicking grown-ups' lives and they're so cute; they're based on the drawings of a young nun. While the Germans were exporting the figurines, they were killing children by the millions. Anything folkish was used by the Nazis for their idea of blood soil and dumb Aryan peasantry, no intellectualism. I made one of them: a little Jew. With a suitcase and a yellow star. My work is very political; it brings the dark side of folk art back. People either love it or they hate it. There are some people who say it doesn't really do anything for them. But there are very few people who say, "This is beautiful."

Writer **Tess Gerritsen** initially avoided drawing on her own cultural background for her art. When she experienced mainstream success, she felt that she was able to tell a story that hit closer to home. "I haven't written a lot about the Asian American experience," she told us.

The reason I haven't is that I was told many years ago by an editor that those books don't sell very well, that Americans were not interested in the Asian American experience. Back then, perhaps, it was true. But now I have had a successful TV show, *Rizzoli and Isles*, and I have a readership and I have two characters who are highly beloved. I thought, maybe now I can risk writing about something closer to my own life. What I did in *The Silent Girl* is introduce three Asian American characters. One of them is a very powerful middle-aged martial arts master, a woman, and because I just love this character, she took over the story. But if I were to put her in a book by herself as the main and only character, I'm not sure it would have sold as well, because readers want Jane Rizzoli and Maura Isles to be center stage.

I think it is a sad commentary about America in a way, or maybe about the majority culture. The majority culture doesn't always care that much about what the minority culture is going through. They have no idea what it's like to be an outsider or to be Black or to be Asian. They have no idea that we see the world in a different way. They have no idea that, when I walk into a room, I am always aware that I'm the only Asian in the room. I'm always thinking, "Who else in here looks like me?" Minorities are always aware that we're minorities. We are always thinking about race, even though we may not talk about it. I tried to address some of that in the book, and I'm not sure that I'll revisit that theme again. This was something of a cathartic book for me, because I introduce an Asian American cop who voices how I felt growing up, being judged because of what I looked like.

Whereas Gerritsen focused on her feelings about ethnic identity within her own lifetime, writer **Gina B. Nahai** took the opportunity to explore her family's cultural history through her art. "In English, my great-grandmother's name was Peacock," she told us.

Literally all the characters in my first novel *Cry of the Peacock* are real people. When I was studying political science, I found out that the Iranian Jews are the oldest Jews in the Diaspora. The history goes back to the time of the destruction of the First Temple. Jews were brought in as slaves to the area that used to be Babylon. But I found out in the 1980s that there is absolutely no record of their existence anywhere. Nobody ever wrote it down. It is mentioned here and there; those old European travelers would mention the Jews of such and such a region in Persia. But that was it. And that, to me, was startling. It took me years to figure out why that was. I thought because of the Iranian Revolution and all these people leaving, it seemed like there would be no Jewish presence left in Iran. I thought this last generation, when they die off there really will be no record of this whole community. I thought that the history should be recorded. I researched and found a book that covered Iran's history for the last 200 years. A lot of my political science and research training went into that part of the history.

Stuck in a Category

Nahai struggled with being pigeonholed because of her background. "When *Cry of the Peacock* came out, your average Westerner didn't know there were Iranian Jews," she said.

When the book came out, I went to a Brentano's in Century City Mall to do a signing, and the manager said, "I don't know where to stock the book. I don't know where to put it under." I said, "What about fiction?" They responded, "What about it? What's an Iranian Jew?" She finally put it under Judaica. I don't know, if a novel comes out about Haitian Jews, where do you put it? I would put it under fiction.

Actress **Ann Harada** had similar experiences in a different area.

When I was younger, I was trying so hard. I told people, "You can cast me in *Miss Saigon*. I can be a bar girl." Of course, I am the least bar-girl person in the world. I would have been horrible. But at the time I felt I could swing it. I was young and felt, "Use me, put me in the back; I don't care." But they weren't interested, and rightly so. Or I tried to be in *The King and I*, and the other traditional shows where you need a whole bunch of Asian people. I'm the most contemporary person you've ever met. It's difficult to imagine that I come from an ancient land and am very formal in my ways. I'm the least ethereal person I know, the least exotic person I've ever met. I'm completely of this time. I think people think, "She's an Asian girl, she could be in these exotic shows." Well, my persona isn't that. I was trying so hard to be something I'm not and it was obviously never going to happen. So most of my work has been nontraditional because people have been able to say, "She's not *that* but she could be the spunky girl or the crazy lady or the wacky something." I don't have a problem auditioning for anybody, if they're interested in seeing *me*. I don't like being brought in if they think, "Oh, we haven't seen an Asian girl yet; let's see Ann." If you have no intention of casting me, let's not go through this. I don't need to do tricks for you. We – I mean, all actors of color – struggle with this on an ongoing basis. There are some parts you're going to get because you're Asian; there are some parts you're not going to get because you're Asian. And there are some parts you're going to get regardless, because of who you are. And those are the parts that you really treasure. I've had an unconventional career. I haven't had that many specifically Asian roles, where the script says, "Asian woman." When people say, "Play Asian" – that's not helpful. You can only play human.

Filmmaker **Steven Okazaki** has also encountered pushback when trying to tell human stories from behind the camera:

My goal has been to make films about the things I care about; to make a living doing it; and to not get stuck in a bracket. From the beginning of my career, I could feel the bracket closing in on me. Being an Asian American filmmaker, people – the programming executives, the funders, other filmmakers, film festivals, viewers, your own community – expect you to make Asian American films. I believe in and support Asian American films and filmmakers. There are so many rich untold stories, so many important issues that aren't addressed, so many clichéd misrepresentations of Asian culture. But I don't want to be told what kinds of films to make. I don't want anybody to think that's all I'm interested in or all I'm capable of. It's insulting. And very hard to escape. ESPN might let you do Bruce Lee or Shohei Otani, but not Joe Montana or Michael Jordan. Not that I'm interested. PBS and Netflix are not that different.

When I made *Black Tar Heroin* for HBO, it was the most difficult subject I could think of, one that everyone seemed afraid to touch. I hoped it would help me break out of the Asian American bracket, to be seen as a filmmaker who could take on any subject. Then I realized I'd only created a new bracket, the hardcore drug filmmaker. But that's the movie world. George Miller was stuck in a Mad Max bracket until he had the power to show what else he was.

Okazaki continued: "People think it's better for Asian American filmmakers these days. Maybe a tiny bit, but not much really. Ask any Asian American filmmaker if it's easier, if the market is more open to them. There might be two directors and two actors in LA who'd say 'yes,' but they're still fighting the bracket."

Political Politeness

Artist **Lex Marie** experienced a different side of being constrained by other people's expectations of someone's art based on their background: the dearth of honest feedback. "A lot of my work is about not just raising a child, but raising a young Black boy in America," she said.

A lot of my work speaks to problems that are so specific to America, whether it is the public school system or the American healthcare system. I think that it's hard for people to critique experiences that they can't relate to themselves or that they don't know much about. A few years ago, I was in a residency in Arlington, Virginia, and I was the only Black resident there. There were no other Black people in the entire building – like nobody. It was an incredible opportunity and everybody there was amazing, but my work during that time was about adultification and how Black children are seen as less innocent. Black boys are treated differently and more mature than their white counterparts; they have a mustache at twelve years old and are seen as men. No one knew how to talk to me about my work, because they didn't want to step on my toes. You know what I mean? But I didn't want that. I wanted to hear honest opinions – what they thought of the work, the actual technique and skill, and also the subject matter. With Black artists in particular, they always say that you have to make works of art about trauma or things that you went through. I don't feel that way at all. It's not my duty. I just feel like I need to, like I'll be doing myself a disservice if I didn't use my art as the outlet it's always been for me. The things that I'm reacting to are the things that are really happening in my life.

Often, art can unite people from all backgrounds. Playwright **Kristoffer Diaz** shared:

I'm fascinated with the dividing lines between groups of people, whatever they are. The idea of what is Latino. That label, Latino, is sometimes really helpful and sometimes really distancing. It takes an entire continent of people who are completely different in terms of specific cultural identities and lumps them into one identity here in the United States. What does that mean and how do you really think about that? It's mind-boggling to think that if you talk about Latino, under that umbrella, you're talking about a Puerto Rican kid from a Jewish neighborhood in New York City, a wealthy Argentinian, a poor Dominican, whatever. I'm not mixed race, my family is one hundred percent Puerto Rican, but my generation was all born in New York. My parents' generation was also born in New York. The difference between living back on the island and living in New York is vast. When I started out, I thought of it as a racial question. When I moved on to college, I started to understand that I wasn't really talking about race, I was talking about ethnicity. Now I'm realizing that it's even less about ethnicity, its more cultural and has a lot to do with economic class.

The differences, I think, are more about class differences than they are race or ethnic differences or anything else. A lot of that has to do with education and a lot of that has to do with financial status. There are so many other things that factor into a person's identity. The things that connect people within a cultural group or class – and the things that may distance people within a class from each other – I'm fascinated with that. For me, the theater is the way to deal with this because the theater is so collaborative that you have to have different points of view mixed into whatever it is that you're working on.

PART V

Reflections

18 | *When Artists Fail*
We're in the failure business

Artists may accept failure. They may acknowledge its inescapability. Many may even see it as a vehicle for growth and development. However, failure is rarely anyone's favorite part of the process. We will try to make it your favorite chapter of the book, though! But if we fail, don't tell us; we know it is inevitable. As writer **Mary Roach** told us, quoting her editor: "Can't have a slam dunk every time."

Even artists we might think are immune may still be concerned. Opera singer-neuroscientist **Indre Viskontas** said,

A lot of the artists whom I look up to as having been very successful – some of them are multi-millionaires from their art – say the same thing: "I don't know where my next job is going to come from. I feel like I'm never going to work again every time I finish a job." I think that's just a struggle for the artist, and it's a very human struggle. I think a lot of people are faced with that. I don't think it's an uncommon feeling for anyone, really, except maybe Mark Zuckerberg.

Everyone fails, but artists might do so on a wider stage. Writer **Tess Gerritsen** shared:

Being a published writer means dealing with bad, sometimes horrible reviews. It's especially painful because reviews are so public. I remember reading comments from a group of schoolteachers that writers should just grow up and develop thick skin, because teachers also get performance reviews and they never complain. But how many of them have their scathing performance reviews published in a newspaper, for all to see? Writers, artists, actors, chefs – they know what it's like to have their creations publicly slammed. It's not fun.

What Is Failure?

Failure can mean different things to different people. Singer-songwriter **Julie Gold** told us:

Failure would only be if I stopped believing in myself. That would be the only thing I would consider failure, if I stopped believing in myself. Because if I had, when I wrote "From a Distance," I lived in one room and I was a secretary. It was rejected for five years. It was unstoppable once it finally won the lotto. But if that hadn't happened, I would still be living in one room, I'd still be a secretary – and I'd still be writing my songs and believing in them as much as I ever did. I just wouldn't have had the notoriety and the, thank God, success that I've had because of "From a Distance." But I would not have considered myself a failure, even at age 55. Because I would still believe in what I was doing and I would still be doing it for love. But if I didn't believe in what I was doing, then I would consider myself a failure.

"Artists think about failure a lot," actor **Michael Kostroff** said.

I don't want to speak for too many people, but I think we worry more about artistic failure than financial failure. I will often take a job that doesn't pay a lot – and I've even done theater for free – because I want to do good art, I want to do good stuff. And when I say good art, I don't mean highfalutin and intellectual. I'm a big fan of things that are just silly and make people laugh, or are lovely diversions. But, I mean, failure to me – I had an experience of failure on *Les Mis*. I had a really, really rough rehearsal period. I've never had anything like it. The director didn't like anything I was doing. I was really kind of brutalized. To tell you the truth, it was traumatic. That's what I describe as failure. Usually, people like my work and they like working with me. This was an unusual experience. And that, to me, is failure. My philosophy with the profession is that failure, in terms of employment, is a given. I talk about this in my workshop, Audition Psych 101. A guy I know is a salesman. And he said, "Michael, you and I are in the same business." I said, "How so? I'm not a salesman." He said, "We're in the failure business. I know when I go on a sales call that the norm is to not make the sale. That's the norm. And I'm in the business of trying to fail less. But I'm still in the failure business." I think that's absolutely true for actors who are auditioning or artists who are trying to make any kind of income from their art. The norm is to fail at that. I don't worry too much about that failure because I am ever willing to make my living in some other way. I don't think that we're entitled to or guaranteed a career. I only know that I *have* to be an artist because that's who I am. I would be tremendously unfulfilled and it would be inauthentic for me to not be an artist. When I'm doing what I do, there's such a sense of hope and lightness. And artists are family to me. We understand each other and it's just such a home base kind of a feeling, I can't explain. It would be tremendously unfulfilling to do anything else.

To musician **Jacob Hyman,** what counts as a failure depends on the intent. "The more concrete the goal, the easier it is to fall short. I guess it all depends on your definition of failure. If I play music and I'm not enjoying it, I feel like I'm failing."

For actor **Doug Jones,** there are several ways in which a seeming failure can be, in fact, a success:

For me, if a project doesn't make money or it doesn't garner awards, that doesn't really mark success or failure for me. Success or failure is when I watch the product myself, am I entertained by it? Am I moved by it? I am not so far off base that I get it wrong. Usually when a project I've been in does entertain me, does move me, and I do connect with it, those tend to be the ones that the public likes, too. That's what's nice about the public response. You have someone to tell you, "Oh good, I wasn't that far off base." For instance, the movie *Hocus Pocus* has become a Halloween classic that families share with each other and kids have grown up with. It's become like *The Wizard of Oz* of Halloween. We made the film in 1993 and they released it in July of that year. A Halloween movie was released in the summer, against all the blockbusters – and it failed miserably at the box office. People were blaming the stars, but I knew that it was ridiculous marketing. It wasn't the product that failed, it was the timing and the advertising that failed. I watched the movie and I was entertained by it. I could see its potential to be a Halloween classic, even though the public wasn't buying it that year. As the years have gone on, the audience has grown every year. We had a success. Then the public finally caught up with that, many years later, when it was released at the right time of year, every year. When I think of personal success and failure, I have a little inner voice when I'm performing in a scene. I know whether it feels real, like I've become this character and I'm living it, or if it feels like I'm putting on a character and I'm performing it. When I feel that click, that connection to the other actors as though the entire crew and the machinery have gone away and we are really living this moment, that's successful to me.

Fear of Failure

Failure may be part and parcel of creative work, but it shouldn't slow you down. Writer-producer **Chris Bearde** said, "You cannot be in comedy and worry about failure. Because you are going to face it. You think about it, but you have to get over it." Actor-composer-artist **Gordon Goodman** agreed. "The more you think about failure, the less you create," he told us. "Thoughts of failure are always hanging around wasting our time. Failure's only failure if you quit. If you've been taught that failure is a disgrace, you'll quit sooner. Your desire to create has to be loud enough to drown out the voice that's saying you might fail."

Focusing too much on failure can be a creativity killer. Filmmaker **Steven Okazaki** told us:

If you worry about failing or what other people think, you can't do the work. For what I do, I need ego and drive, but with as much objectivity as possible. Unlike painting, I don't make films for myself, but for the viewer. When I'm making the film, I'll listen to anyone's opinion unless it's too positive or too negative or it's coming from some movie business hack who wants to turn your script about real-life heroin addicts into a zombie movie. Feedback is important, but you have to know how to process it.

Some metrics of failure, however, can truly impact an artist's future. As a result, it may be impossible to avoid thinking about the prospect entirely. "I think the specter of failure is really used to terrorize writers these days, especially fiction writers," novelist **Susan Choi** said.

Even the people with the best intentions who are on the side of literary fiction, they often talk about failure. Literary publishing is a strange enterprise. Books are never selling as much as people wish they would. Many conversations with my publishers are less about the book than about when should we publish it so that it might get attention so that somebody might buy it. How can we keep this thing from sinking without a ripple? So when the conversation is about how to stave off extreme failure, it's hard not to be preoccupied by failure.

Even when failure cannot be ignored, it shouldn't be internalized. Writer **Susan Breen** told us:

Thinking about failure and rejection is a big thing. As a creative person, you have to get used to the fact that rejection isn't personal. And that's a hard thing. I don't take rejection well, to put it mildly. I know it's a part of the job. I know you're going to get negative critiques. I know that it happens. But it's hard. To me, it's the hardest part of the whole thing.

In addition to not taking failure personally, it is also good to have healthy ways of regaining equilibrium. Actress **Ann Harada** has her own routine that helps her. "Sometimes it doesn't matter how much experience you have or what ability you have," she said.

If you're the right look or the right type or the right accent, you get hired. When I'm feeling burnt out, I need to just be very quiet and by myself for a few days and recharge and do nothing but read English murder mysteries and lie on my bed. Because, for me, that's the way to get away from the demands of the world and think: "What is it that you really want to do? What do you want to be spending your time on?"

Coping with Failure

Some setbacks require solutions that are bigger in scope. Dancer-psychologist **Paula Thomson** told us:

When I was very young, teachers and friends recognized me as a dancer, but my father wanted me to focus on swimming, so I stopped formal training in dance and returned to it later. I always loved dance and my mother shared my love and encouraged me to continue, which I did secretly without my father's knowledge. Because I suppressed my desire to dance, and more specifically to choreograph dances, I missed many opportunities as a young adolescent. When I fully returned to dance, my creative impulses were muted, and it took several years of painful exploration to find my voice. This required entering therapy, addressing my own childhood trauma, and finding the courage to create dances that were generated from within me. I am also hypermobile, so I had many knee injuries which meant time away from dancing to heal – but not time away from choreographing.

There is coping with failure, and then there is using it as a vehicle for growth. Photographer **Greg Friedler** said,

I know what my failures were. So the next time that sort of opportunity presents itself, I have a much better chance of being successful because I've already done that image. I know how to clean it up or make it more minimal or make it more colorful or something like that. The lesson learned from trying to capture it, that's what photography is – it's a very strange way of collecting, of capturing. There will be many images that just won't work but then when I look at them, I do a mental inventory of what it's about and why it failed and whether I am overreacting: Is it really a failure? The next time, I will be better equipped. I'll give you an example of that: There are a couple of old bridges near here, these old iron bridges with funky colors that aren't used anymore. On a sunny day, I went out and photographed them. When I looked at the photos, I thought "God, these are really awful for so many reasons." They needed to be more minimalistic and this and that. They were just kind of splotchy. There was a shadow. Somehow it occurred to me that what they needed was an overcast sky, so that the sky would be white and the bridge would stand out more as a real graphic object. The next time

I went out, it was completely overcast and I got great photos. Everything just fell into place.

For musician **Jim Tobbe,** failure propelled him to compose, rather than just perform. "I learned to play guitar the wrong way, and I still play it the wrong way," he said.

I'm left-handed, and I play basically upside down and backwards. It was just the way I picked it up as a kid and by the time I got too deep into it, I couldn't change. Part of the handicap with learning the wrong way is that everybody wanted me to learn how to play guitar the right way. I didn't take any music theory. It was easier for me to write my own music instead of learning how to play other people's music.

Actor-composer-artist Gordon Goodman summed it up neatly: "I never thought it was a disgrace to fail. Failure's probably the most organic route to achieving anything."

Finally, failure can serve as a motivator. "Most people will say, 'I never really think about fear, I only think about success,'" writer-actor **Jim Piddock** told us.

But I think fear and failure are important. I think successful people are driven because they're frightened of being poor again or failing. I think it drives you to excellence. I don't know if it drives you to be a creative person; that's very different. But if you are so inclined and want to be as good as you can, then the fear of failure should light a fire under your ass. It shouldn't become a paralyzing agent. I think creative people need to be allowed to fail along the way in the creative process. Fear of failure is in the final product. That's the fear that I certainly have. That's important. I don't want what I do to be crap.

Failure may be one way that artists can be motivated, but it is not the only one. As we will discover in the next chapter, mentors can shape and nurture artists – and inspire them to be mentors, themselves.

19 | *Inspiring Creativity in Others*
I want people to have the same joy I have

You may have noticed that we covered teachers in the first part of our book ("Childhood"). Chapter 4 ("School through an Artist's Eyes") addressed how artists can be treated differently – and not necessarily better – in school because of their talents, and Chapter 5 ("School Struggles") focused on terrible teachers. We saved the stories of amazing educators and mentors for this chapter because, as you will see, marvelous teachers can not only inspire artists to create but also to themselves give back and mentor young artists later in life.

Some teachers use an artist's passion to teach them core concepts in other disciplines. Writer-producer **Marianna Mott Newirth** said,

As a child, I grew up with a learning disability, so already I was backwards. I would reverse letters, I would reverse numbers, I would reverse numerical concepts; I was finally diagnosed with dyscalculia. In fifth grade, I was really struggling with long division. I just didn't get it. You've got these numbers and you've got this box over them. It didn't make any sense to me, because I was looking at something different. Maybe I was looking at the structure of the lines. But I had this wonderful tutor. She was an extraordinary woman and knew I was very interested in dance. One day, she took masking tape and taped a giant long division problem to the floor. We choreographed our way through long division. I learned it was okay to approach something from a completely different point of view from other people.

Inspiration from Aspiration

Other teachers inspire by example. "I had one teacher in particular who was really, really important to me," novelist **Diana Abu-Jaber** told us.

I studied with him my last year in high school. He loved poetry. I remember he brought a friend in who was a poet herself and had her read to the class. That was *so* exciting to me. I loved just meeting a poet. Listening to her read, listening to her words. And then he read to us a lot. I remember he read long passages from *The Wasteland*. He read a lot of T. S. Eliot, he read Sylvia Plath. I hadn't really read any poetry before that class. I remember feeling like the top of my head was coming off and that was spectacular. He also had us write. He had us write short stories and poetry and so it gave us permission to look at our writing as something serious, something that was valuable, worthwhile.

Visual artist/musician **Tine Kindermann** remembered:

The art in school was always very boring until high school. I had one art teacher who I adored. He was a very quiet man. We were all totally arrogant and dissing Raphael because we thought he was kitschy, and then the teacher would just say, "Look at over here, how Raphael handles the wrappings and the light and shadow." He taught us how to look.

Discovering Hidden Talents

Teachers can also be early advocates who recognize an artist's nascent ability. "Having a talent at writing as a kid isn't the kind of thing that people necessarily notice," writer **Peggy Orenstein** told us.

Not in the way that they would notice somebody who was outstanding on the piano or an amazing artist like my husband [Steven Okazaki], who was seen as special because he could draw. I don't think that that's the case with writing because everybody is supposed to be able to write, even if you don't like it or kind of suck at it. Within my family, my brothers were also imaginative, gifted writers, so it wasn't seen as something unusual or exceptional. It was just expected. I was neither critiqued nor overpraised. In school, I started getting more positive feedback around sixth grade, and that was meaningful to me. Then my eighth-grade English teacher had us each make a book of our original poems. On the last page of mine, she wrote, "Get in touch with me when you're a famous writer." That was the first time someone suggested that idea to me. I still have her note, and I've actually tried to find her to thank her, but no luck.

Actress **Ann Harada** had a similar experience:

In about seventh grade, they picked me out of the choir and my music teachers could tell that I could sing. I didn't know that. They said you have a really nice voice; you should train and think about singing. I was very awkward and ungainly as a child – very unattractive and just flat-out homely. I was at my most ugly duckling stage. It turned out that I really was musical and I could hear harmony. I thought, oooh – this is what I like.

This is what I'm actually good at, as opposed to writing and drawing. At that point, I completely gave myself over to wanting to sing and perform.

Perhaps at the pinnacle are those teachers who are true full-service mentors. Singer-songwriter **Julie Gold** remembered:

My first-grade teacher suggested that my parents try me on piano lessons. I remember the day my piano teacher came and sat down with me and tested me. The first thing she did, she pointed out middle C, checked my hands on the piano to see how long they were, and took me on as a student. The time I spent with my piano teacher was so intense that I don't sit at the piano without having her next to me. On my right. Every day. If I was learning something new, she'd pat it on my back rhythmically. Lovingly. Or she'd play it, the upper register with her right hand, with me. I was never alone.

For writer-performance artist **Annie Lanzillotto,** Catholic school did not inspire her creativity until she encountered a nun who not only recognized her talent but kept mentoring her across disciplines.

When I started seventh grade, there was a nun who ran the oratory team. She said to me in class one day, "Lanzillotto, you have a big mouth; come to my room after school today." She gave me the Gettysburg Address to memorize. That began a two-year relationship with this nun; it was really a creative process because she was a theater director in her soul. She taught me how to gesture, how to have intention, how to compose myself in front of an audience, how to memorize – the basic tools of acting. She flattened out my Bronx accent on words like America and beauty. She got rid of the Bronx when I was preparing for a competition. We won all sorts of trophies and I won the state championship. She taught me what you do if you forget your lines in front of an audience. We practiced failure, we practiced success, we practiced respect. She would bring me to little gatherings and to parades to honor people and I would have to give speeches. From there, we went on to having me write the speeches. Even now, she remains one of the best theater directors I ever had. She was able to elevate my abilities into a performance. That experience taught me what it was like to move a crowd, to ride a crowd like you were on a surfboard, with the ups and the downs and they're with you with every breath, they laugh, they cry, they gag.

Learning to Trust

The final lesson that actress **Donna Lynne Champlin**'s favorite college professor taught her was particularly powerful:

I absolutely worshipped her. She walked on water for me, could do no wrong and all I wanted was her approval. I had done a play and I felt very solid about the work I had done, especially on the night she had seen it. I went to her office to ask for her critique and she ripped me to shreds. Absolutely ripped me to shreds. The worst part was not even that she didn't like my work. It was the conflict between my own gut telling me that my work was good and her telling me it wasn't which threw me into a complete tailspin for over a year. I was confused at my very core. It was devastating – not that I couldn't trust her anymore – but that I couldn't trust *myself* anymore. That was the blow I couldn't recover from. I developed stage fright. I slid back in class. I became timid at rehearsals. My work became constipated and cowardly. Finally, she pulled me aside and said, "Kid! What's the matter with you? Every day you get worse and worse, with more and more fear." I told her that ever since she told me my work was "shit" (an actual quote) I felt lost. I *was* lost. I had no center, no instincts, no gut anymore. And she literally laughed and said, "Oh, kid. I am an old woman! What do I know? There is no one more important than you. If your work is pure and you know it, then what do you care what I think?"

Then she winked at me. I realized then that she had done the whole thing on purpose to test me. To make me stop looking for validation everywhere outside myself – especially in her, because she wasn't going to be down the hall from me my whole life. But *I* would always be with me, right? So, she told me my work was shit when she knew I *knew* it wasn't, to see if I had the stones to believe myself over her. I failed and wasted a year being lost, but it's a lesson I've never forgotten. To be clear, it's not that I feel I am beyond all criticism and direction. On the contrary, I love it when a director suggests I try something else and my gut jumps up and down in agreement. That's like Christmas. But that sacred place inside me, where my creative truth lives? It doesn't get touched by anyone else anymore. It's totally safe now. Because I protect it.

Opera singer-neuroscientist **Indre Viskontas** explained how, in opera, there are entire ecosystems comprised of many mentors to help a young singer grow. "It takes a village to raise an opera singer," she said.

Every opera singer has both a voice teacher and a coach. A voice teacher has taught you how to sing since you were little. They often used to be opera singers. More often than not, as your career develops and your voice changes, you go with more and more advanced teachers. The teacher talks about the technical aspects of singing, like is your diaphragm loose enough to support all the air that needs to move through your vocal cords in such a way that it's free and easy and creates the right sound. The coach is a pianist or conductor who runs through music with you and helps you develop an interpretation of a piece. The coach is often versed in whatever genre of opera you are specializing in or are currently singing. You have Baroque coaches, Mozart coaches, Verdi coaches. Some coaches are expert in many different areas. You do your technical work with your teacher and your interpretive work with your coach.

You continue to have that training throughout the lifespan of your career, because what you hear in your own head is not what the audience hears. You hear the sound through the bones of your face, and that's not what other people's ears hear. So it's hard to tell when something is sounding bad, to a certain extent. Eventually, you develop a knowledge of what it feels or sounds like to you when it's right. It's so important to have a great teacher because they can hear the strain that you're putting on your voice before you feel it. Maybe you're doing a production where they're having you sing one part of the aria while you're lying down and it feels fine to you – except all of a sudden, on the fourth night of the performance, you've lost your voice. A good teacher will come to your rehearsal and listen to what you're doing and say, "Actually, you know what, when you're lying down and you're doing that, I can hear that you're putting a little bit of pressure on your soft palate and if you don't get rid of that, you're going to have problems later on." Singing is an athletic ability in that way because any golf pro is going to continue to have coaches; every baseball team has pitching coaches and batting coaches to make sure that everything's going well for you. You need all these people around you in order to help you sustain that.

Learning to Pass the Baton

Perhaps the final legacy of an amazing mentor is helping artists realize the joy and value of passing on that support to the next generation. Actor-writer-record producer **Bruce Kimmel** told us:

When I was in my first year at college, I saw the musical *The Most Happy Fella* with its original star, Robert Weede. This show was a life-changer and Weede gave one of the greatest performances I've ever seen to this day on any stage. There was a big tent where the performers had their dressing rooms and I went back there after the show. I was just so emotional and I said, "I need to meet Robert Weede" and they took me back to him. He was the kindest and warmest person. When he found out I was an actor, he was so encouraging and sweet to me. It was unbelievable. He invited me to be his guest at the cast party. He kept me with him that entire party and introduced me to everybody, including the director, whom I ended up auditioning for six months later, and who cast me. The graciousness of Weede, making sure everyone at this party knew me and knew I was an actor and knew how in love with the business I was. I had never seen anything like that before or since – and that's how I live. When I started being a record producer, I had people who were obsessive about the albums I produced. They would write me or come to meet me very timidly and I'd say, "If you're ever in New York and you want to come to a session, let me know." And they would take me up on that. When I was directing movies, I would have an open set. That's the way I am with people who take the time to write or talk to you. I just want to be like Robert Weede. You never want to be negative with a young person starting out; it can be devastating. You read about people who are terse with their fans and I don't get it. I would never live like that – all because of Robert Weede.

The journey to become a teacher can be a winding road for an artist. Novelist **T. Coraghessan Boyle** said,

I've been teaching since I was twenty-one years old and it became a part of my life. I didn't want to be a teacher. I didn't know about being a teacher. It just happened, sort of accidentally. I sort of grew into it. I've always had a lot of energy and great commitment to what I'm doing and it has been very, very good for me in that it keeps me out of the house and enables me to maybe for at least a day bury some of the problems I've got with a given work. All of the time I would spend at the University of Southern California, I would be teaching and with my students, and that's good. In my most difficult period, which hasn't been for a long, long time, I would teach a full load, so that would be two days a week. That would add up to something like fifty-four days a year. It's not exactly grueling. I just love talking about art with young writers who are just like me and have the same desires and talents. I believe in this art and love it so much and it's great to see what an enormous pool of talent there is for this particular art form. Even though, of course, in our technologically obsessed society and visually oriented society, it has a smaller slice of the apple. You go back to Dickens's time when he was the only show in town, and he'd perform. People wanted the serials, this was their TV, their movies, their live play. But we don't have that. Writers are far less important these days. It doesn't mean that we're any less devoted. We do what we're going to do, no matter what.

Learning by Teaching

As Boyle noted, mentors often gain a great deal from working with students. "I'm always inspired by the exuberance of younger writers," novelist **Chang-rae Lee** said.

It reminds me of the passion I had at the beginning, all that ambitious energy propelling you to write deep into the early hours. Of course, it's very different now. I wake up, make coffee and have breakfast with my wife, and then I head to my study. I sit there for as long as I'm able. But being with my students, and also writers, especially the ones early in their careers, reminds me of the essential spark of the practice.

For visual artist **Lex Marie,** the process of teaching was the most valuable: "I think I learned more about myself as an artist through teaching than I did from being a student. I think things have to be more engrained in your head to teach it, rather than consume it. I had to keep practicing, because I was teaching it to students."

Mentoring young artists has its own challenges. For example, it can be hard to create without years of life to draw on. As novelist **Susan Choi** told us,

It's hard if you're young and you want to write; you don't have any experience. Not much has happened to you, and you don't know much about anything. I teach students now and my students write these stories about parents losing children to illness. I didn't even try to do that. I should have done more of that. When I was fifteen, I should have just written about how it felt to be fifteen. But that always seemed so lame. You don't realize you're not going to be fifteen for very long. Before long you're not going to remember anything about what it was really like. I don't remember any of my real thoughts or feelings. I can vaguely remember, but I don't remember how it really, mentally felt to be that age. You supersede yourself; your forty-seven-year-old self is going to erase a lot of that.

Novelist **Robert Olen Butler** notes that young artists may need to dig deep to find their voice. He told us:

There are no prodigies in literature, there are no Mozarts, because the sophisticated and nuanced command of language is a fairly advanced skill, and as a child, one doesn't have that. Also, you're required as a literary artist to have an unconscious that is full of life experience. As a child, one's life experience is very limited. Literary writers have authentic command of their literature, of the things that are no longer active and are fixed as literal memories. They have to dissolve themselves into what I've called the dream space, or the white-hot center of the unconscious, if you want to use a Freudian term. As a child, that doesn't yet exist very much, or not at all. Even for young adults. I have trouble with my undergraduates in the sense that I teach them that they have to go into their unconscious to create the kind of works they aspire to. Many of them aspire to create literature, but they haven't lived enough yet and they haven't forgotten enough yet. It seems to me that a child would be drawn to the visual form or, in other cases, an audio form because in those modes of artistic expression the primary creative medium doesn't require a richly developed unconscious.

Costume designer **Michael Krass** looks for a certain confidence in his students:

What you want a kid to say is, "Let me try it my way." I respect students enormously because something in them said, "I think I want to be in theater." Meaning, I need attention; meaning, I have something creative; meaning, I don't want to be like everybody else; meaning, there's something about people that interests me – humanness or emotion. That's how they land in the building. Then we spend four years asking, "How's that useful to somebody? Yes, you're right, but now how could that be useful to other people?"

Giving Yourself Permission

A good teacher also needs confidence. Novelist Diana Abu-Jaber said:

Teaching in a creative writing workshop, the students push that question: What gives me the right to tell this story? What gives you the right to teach it? They want credentials. I realized that, if I wanted to be a successful teacher, then I had to own that identity. I had to say, yes, this is who I am. Because if I didn't claim it, the students weren't going to respect it. That's when it happened, when I had to take it on as a professional identity.

Musician **Bruce Mack** helps teachers gain confidence when they guide young artists. "I've worked with all kinds of teachers," he said.

Many are searching for various ways to teach their kids but didn't have a way of connecting with them. To this day, many have the skills but are uncomfortable initiating a lesson. I show them different types of exercises I use for music lessons and workshops, such as getting people in a group to coax them into being expressive with their voice without demonstrating any ability to sing, but just being expressive and having fun. That builds up student confidence and introduces them to their abilities, even though they haven't been asked to show any real skill. I try to show teachers how to be creative in their teaching. For instance, first we have to learn how to play together in rhythm, keep a beat. Once we do that, the next plan of action would be to give three or four people, who are comfortable keeping the beat, a sound or instrument to mimic; one might be piano, another maybe bass, and so on. Then I allow them to suggest another sound, but I'll say hold that idea, we're going to get to that – for now, everyone else will keep the beat.

That's the first goal. Now they're drawn in and interested in the lesson because they see where it's going. The attempt to mimic another instrument or sound becomes fun. This is where a connection happens, the teacher can now improvise within the lesson to find the best teaching approach for these participants and a group dynamic has been identified.

Mentoring doesn't always happen in a classroom. Photographer **J. Cleary Rubinos** explained:

When you're starting out, you should probably apprentice under somebody. Everybody needs a little art mentor in their life. You can bounce ideas off of them. I found the idea of being mentored quite lovely and very cost-effective instead of art school. You learn what's expected of you. Like not to forget to take a picture of the flowers when taking photographs of weddings; the couple spent a lot of money on those. Don't forget to take a picture of the table cards; they spent a lot of money on those. There are little things you need to remember. I've reached a point where people ask me questions about how to go through a wedding day and not freak out. They ask my advice.

Sometimes, mentoring happens in a spontaneous moment. "If I'm on a plane, I'll draw a person's face and give it to them," actor-writer-artist **Gordon Goodman** told us.

If I'm doing a show, I'll draw a person's face in the cast and give it to them. People will inevitably say, "Oh, I can never draw," or "I wish I could draw." They're just lying to me – lying, lying, lying – and to themselves as well. So, I start by showing them some of the tricks of drawing, gimmicks. You realize that the distance between two eyes, for instance, is another eye. A third eye. You can divide their face into halves or thirds and can measure the distance of a person's nose based on that. You can set the fingers maybe six or seven inches above the knee. Everything's in relationship. It's all a gimmick. Creativity is filled with gimmicks. When you put them all together, things start to take shape. So that's what I tell people, "Art's a bunch of gimmicks. Anybody can do it if you learn the gimmicks." The real artistic expression for me comes later with shading and color, adding values. That's where I feel the emotion enter into the work.

Inspiring Inspiration

Visual artist-entrepreneur **Phyllis Brody** devoted her career to helping the youngest artists blossom and discover their creativity:

One of the most exciting things for me is seeing somebody intently involved in creating. And if that situation has been instigated by something I've given them – a product that they bought or a class or an experience that I've set up – I love that. I want people to have the same joy I have experimenting and creating. That's the essence of what we were trying to do with Creativity for Kids. It's not the carefully colored in the lines thing that we were aiming for; it's about feeling absolutely terrific about making something uniquely your own. I know they're only craft kits, but there's some real sentiment behind them and on a level it's pretty powerful and spiritual because it touches on the universal, timeless need that humans have to create. The person is at the center of the creative experience, not the project.

20 | *Looking Backward, Looking Forward*
I've left enough of a thumbprint on the world

We started with the artists' childhood, from the influence of family to school experiences. We discussed how our artists first found their calling, whether it was a sudden epiphany or a gradual wave of insight. Next came stories of artists finding their place in their chosen world and, for some, hitting it big. Then we explored the realities of an artist's life – the toll on relationships, the struggle to make a living, and how their art has shaped who they are. In this section, we've talked about failures and inspirations – and now, finally, we see how our artists look back on their careers and consider what they will leave behind.

Writer **Susan Breen**'s career has been a source of joy:

I have always loved reading, and I've always felt like writers were a supreme sort of being. To be a part of this world is all I ever wanted to do. I just didn't think I could do it. Whatever my little toehold is in this world, I get a kick out of it. It never gets old to me to see my book in a bookstore. I can't imagine really doing anything else. I go into my little world and I am happy there and tell my story. My favorite people, other than my family, are other writers. I know there are people who say, "I'm going to write a novel. I'm going to be a novelist." I didn't think that in college. I thought, "I'm going to be a reporter." I'm sort of dumbfounded that this is where the journey took me.

Photographer **Greg Friedler** had an equally positive view. "I think I'm happy with my body of work," he said.

I think it's remarkable. I'm forty years old and I'm probably going to be making photographs for another forty-five years. I don't see it ending – it's too big a love affair. A lot of artists get spurts of creativity for two years or twelve months and that's all they really do. Then other people have it for their whole lives. Mine is sort of a love affair. If I don't think about photography every day of my life, I feel like something is missing.

Tragically, Friedler would not get another forty-five years to share his gifts with the world. He passed away only a few years after talking to us, and we mourn his loss.

When artists consider their earlier work, they can have a variety of often conflicting feelings. "Sometimes I feel good about my work, more often not," novelist **Chang-rae Lee** told us.

Often, I feel like I could have done so much more, both in the contemplation before the writing and writing itself, and then at other moments I think I couldn't have done any more. I don't reread my novels – I don't need to. I know them. My opinions about them fluctuate. Sometimes I think I was successful with a certain book, and then at other moments I'll feel like I left a lot on the table. It's never one emotion.

Similarly, writer-musician **Cecil Castellucci** said,

If I were to go back and rewrite my first novel, it would be totally different. It is just a document of where I was as an artist at that time. I'm very proud of it. I read it and I don't cringe. But I see it as a very naive and juvenile work. I wouldn't make the same choices now that I did then. You just keep evolving. I don't think I'll ever be satisfied. I don't think when I'm 100 years old, I'll think, "I've finally done it."

Other times, what is most salient is one's consistency. "I feel like I've been doing the same shit all my life," musician-theater artist **Steve Riffkin** said.

None of it has ever felt any different. I just got increasingly better paid for it. There's no journey to speak of, as far as I'm concerned. It's just been one long path of the same stuff. I think about the teacher that I was when I started and I'm not that much better now. I was pretty darned good when I started doing it all those years ago. There were no major epiphanies, nothing where the light went on. This was always what I was going to do. I don't think anybody who knows me would have thought I was going to do anything else. That's pretty much what I got when I went to reunions: "Of course that's what you're doing."

Rethinking Career Decisions

Major decisions, such as whether or not to pursue advanced study in a creative field, can be a source of reflection later in life, even for successful artists. Novelist **Susan Choi** wonders what might have happened if she had pursued graduate school later in life. "I got an MFA from Cornell University," she said.

It was a great program, but it wasn't that helpful for me personally. I wasn't ready; even though I was looking forward to being a real writer, I was still really young. I hadn't been out of school long enough and I was trying to get serious, but I just didn't have what it took to be left alone in a room with my writing. I entered the program expecting to be turned into a writer. But I couldn't let someone else figure it out for me; I had to figure it out for myself. It was really hard and I was very unproductive while I was a student. I just couldn't figure out what my subject was, I couldn't find a project. I was rudderless. I think I ended up succeeding as a writer through a series of stages. Grad school was one of them. But in grad school I wasted a lot of time and I regret it. I wish I'd spent my twenties traveling and doing more eclectic, weird, experience-building things instead of trying so hard to be professional and ending up sort of cutting my life off at the knees. I went back to school too quickly. In the short time between being a college student and being a graduate student, I wandered around, really just lost. I lived in five cities and held a series of minimum-wage jobs. I was a cashier here and a waitress there and if a friend of mine said, "I'm going to move to this city," I'd say, "Okay, I'll go, too." And that was kind of great, actually, and I wish I'd done more of it, but at the time, it felt too scary. It wasn't secure enough. My parents weren't thrilled. I had student loans to pay. So I hastened my way back to school. Now I have two kids and I feel like, "Why didn't I backpack through Southeast Asia, why didn't I go to Guatemala, why didn't I do all those things?" When I was twenty-two, I was just too timid. Now I think, I wish I had done more irresponsible, crazy, youthful stuff. But I also don't regret going to grad school, because if I hadn't, I would have always thought, "Maybe I should go to grad school." So, I got it over with early.

In contrast, muralist **David Guinn** wonders what an alternate path, in which he went to graduate school, might have looked like:

There is a piece that I feel like I've missed by not going to art school; I actually applied to grad school, but decided not to go. I felt at the time that I would not make back the cost of the tuition. However, what I missed was an education in how to be an artist. I've had to figure that out for myself which hasn't been easy. I've learned a lot doing murals. I feel like my work has changed a lot. I was pushed a lot, forced to be rigorous by working in public. People say, "Why did you do that? Why is this?" Everybody's always asking questions, which I guess is what would happen in art school.

For actor-composer-artist **Gordon Goodman**, his "what if" moment was an onstage accident. "I'd had this huge, beautiful, heroic classical baritone voice," he told us.

It was the one creative outlet that I loved more than anything else. As long as I had that, I had no fear of the future. My voice was my identity. I'd stand in back of an orchestra, in front of a huge choir, with the conductor in front, and I'd open my mouth and with the first notes that came out, everyone in the orchestra would turn around, straining their necks to look at me. It was so big and rich and beautiful. I would blow everyone away without trying. That sounds conceited but it was true. And that feeling is addictive. I did plenty of things before the accident, of course. I was the first live-action Aquaman. I helped develop the stage persona of Gaston for Disney's *Beauty and the Beast.* Then one summer, I had an accident during a fight scene and crushed my larynx. It changed my voice forever. My identity was gone. It was like a vacuum. I miss singing more than anything.

But if musical theater and singing had continued, I probably wouldn't have had time for a lot of other stuff. I got my PhD in psychology. Completed a large, published research study. I began painting heavily. Got a broker's license. A black belt in karate. I wrote scripts and scores for musicals, hundreds of songs. I have my own animatronic character in a major Disney amusement park. I've worked in television gameshow development. I've taught at a university and colleges. We're thrown curves in life all the time, based on probabilities we can't anticipate. It used to be whenever something in music, or while sculpting, or painting went wrong, I'd say out loud, "Okay, what now?" I always believed there was a way out, a way to still make it work. What can you do but go on? Just say, "Okay, what now?" Not a bad bumper sticker for an artist.

Thinking about the Future Self

How might age impact one's perspective on their career? Actress **Ann Harada** was able to imagine her future self:

There's a point in your life when your voice changes, and maybe I'll use some of those qualities. Hopefully, by the time I'm eighty-five, it won't matter what kind of voice I have. I can still do character parts with a creaky, icky voice. But dancers – their bodies betray them as they age. They have to figure out what kind of career they're going to have. At some point, they have to switch from being dancers to becoming teachers, coaches, choreographers, or whatever.

Meanwhile, legendary singer **Country Joe McDonald** mused on his own career. "People retire at a certain age, generally speaking," he said.

Some people don't; they just keep on going. You only hear about the people who continue to create and work, because they're in the media. They keep on going and keep on creating and then they die. But me, there've been periods when I've been very productive and very successful and periods where I've not. Now, it's kind of over. Priorities change. I have a couple little things, participating in benefits, but I'm considering not performing anymore for a complete professional show. If it's local and it's a benefit and a cause and if I want to, maybe. But if I don't want to, I'm not going to do it. I have nothing to prove anymore. I'm not driven to express a certain thought. The reason to create has diminished. I have thirty albums and I have five kids. There've been times when I thought my output was dwindling and I was not getting stroked as much as I used to. I felt like a has-been, but there's a kind of acceptance. Everybody gets their moment, and I got a lot of fifteen minutes. I've been very, very lucky. I did some stuff that was at the right time and the right place and appreciated, and I think it brought some happiness into people's lives and educated them in some way. It enabled me to have a career and pay the bills and, hey, wow, what a gift. I started doing it for fun and I discovered very early on that I could do it and make money. I could either work in construction and make this money or I could make music and make money. Now, I look at myself and look on the internet and look at books and they've got quotes on me. I never could have imagined that back when I was thinking about what my professional name would be as a trombonist.

Why We Create

Why do artists create in the first place? Such a big question might be a bit beyond our current scope (or the number of pages we have left); however, one reason is to find and maintain meaning in life (Kapoor & Kaufman, 2020; Kaufman, 2018, 2023). Most conceptions of meaning have three parts (Martela & Steger, 2016). One, coherence, is the ability to look back on one's life and make sense of it – as our artists have done by talking to us in the first place. Another, significance, is feeling as though one matters and one's life is worth living. The third, purpose, is having goals and directions for the future, which can include considering one's legacy for future generations (Lifton, 1979, 2011).

"I'm fanatically devoted to what I do," novelist **T. Coraghessan Boyle** told us.

It is my all and everything. Are there dangers to this? Of course there are, and I'm aware of them all. But what if you can't do it anymore? Maybe you lose the ability, the sharpness, the desire. Maybe you repeat yourself. The funny thing with me is every time I come up with an idea for a story, I think, wow – wait a minute, I've already written that one. So I think you would become bereft if it was your whole life, like Hemingway when he was unable to do it. That's the danger of devoting yourself singly to anything. But, again, it's a small danger compared to what human life is and the uselessness of it, really – the uselessness of any endeavor. I used to think that literature was important, that I was important, that the world was important. Of course, I've been disabused of all of these notions. And now I make art in order to satisfy myself and have something to do in life. You've got to find something to live with, something to fill your time. The thing that I've chosen enables me to try to analyze the world. I need to do that. I need to find a reason why. And art enables me to try to do that.

Actor **Doug Jones** is able to appreciate his past work while still being excited for what is to come:

If I got hit by a bus today and it all had to end, I would be very satisfied that I've had a long and very full career. I still have a lot coming, but if it did have to end today, I find I've left enough of a thumbprint on the world with the work I leave behind. If you ask me if I feel like I've arrived? No, I'll never feel like I've arrived until I'm dead and in heaven and meeting my maker. Until then, there's a lot of work to do. I want to keep getting better, I want to meet new challenges, I want to overcome the next hill. But if I had to stop today, I'm not going to begrudge that I didn't get to go forward. I would go, "Oh, wow, look at all we did. It's been a great ride."

What happens when artists think about their legacies? Having any creation preserved so that it might survive you is a reason to be proud. Actor-writer **Jim Piddock** shared:

To get a film made is a miracle. For a film to be good is a double miracle; it's like winning the lottery twice. And if it makes a lot of money, then it's a trifecta of miracles! It's very difficult and a lot of things I've been involved with haven't ended up the way I wanted them to. There's not an awful lot out there that I go "Wow, that's great. I'll be proud of that on my deathbed." But the good news is you only need one gem to leave a legacy in professional terms. Sasha Baron Cohen has done an incredible amount of great work, but if he never does anything ever again, *Borat* will still be remembered as one of the funniest and most innovative comedies of all time. And going a lot further back, if all Oscar Wilde ever wrote was *The Importance of Being Earnest*, it was an enduring legacy. You don't need to be Shakespeare. Just to have one, one great piece of work, and you should be able to say, "My work here is done." Of course, that doesn't happen and we keep striving to do more because that's the way we are.

Opera singer-neuroscientist **Indre Viskontas** considers the difference in legacies between tackling a classic role and creating a new one. "My dream, my what-do-you-want-to-be-when-you-grow-up image of myself was singing in great operas that were 150 years old in big, classic productions," she said.

What I've learned is that, because singers have done these operatic roles for hundreds of years, there's a lot less room for creativity and interpretation. When you're reprising a role that has been performed probably hundreds of thousands of times, such as Mimi in *La Bohème*, if you've read what other people have said about it and watched what other people have done, then you have a richer toolbox from which to draw. However, it's possible that you fall into the trap of mimicry and get stuck in the rut of listening to recordings and seeing people who've done it before. It's very easy to just do what everybody else thinks you should be doing and try to please the crowd, rather than really going out on your own and doing something that comes from your heart. I think you have to work harder at making it your own with a unique perspective. It's like interpreting Shakespeare; it's been done so many times and so many different ways.

The operas that I mainly do now are new compositions. When you're doing an entirely new role, by definition, no one has done it before. It's much easier to do something innovative with a new role than with a role that's been done a thousand times. In a lot of ways, the stakes are a lot lower. When people go see *La Bohème*, they go because they've seen it before or they have a recording of Maria Callas singing Mimi, which they adore, and they want to get immersed in the story. When they go see *The Bonesetter's Daughter*, an opera based on an Amy Tan novel, they're going to see something completely new. They don't know what to expect. They don't know what the music will sound like. You have more room there to do something that the audience enjoys and is also creative. But you might have a really creative performance of Mimi that is not critically acclaimed; people might hate it because it's so different. Whereas if you have a very creative performance of a new role, people might hate it as well, but at least you're given respect for having done something completely new. When I create the role, literally – because no one else has ever done it – I also interact with the composers and can influence the work itself. In that way, I can have a legacy that's beyond "She was a great interpreter of one of Bellini's characters." I can leave a mark on the work itself, rather than just being another interpreter. That feels much more rewarding, though my love for the classics and traditional opera is still very strong. It probably gives me the most joy just on a moment-to-moment basis, but what gives me the most artistic satisfaction is working with the composers. I have a very natural and rational fear of death and of being insignificant in the world. One of the ways that I feel I can have a legacy is through influencing the direction of a particular work of music.

Of course, art can also be purely ephemeral, and the magic of that single moment is its own legacy. "There's a reason that musical theater is so precious," actress Ann Harada said.

You do it and it's done. The only people who see the show are you, your fellow actors, and the people in the audience. It's such a transient medium. We're going to start at 8 o'clock, and then at 10:15 we're going to be done. And we are the only people who are going to know what happened here tonight. It's not there for the ages. Even when you record a play, you weren't physically there. You weren't in the audience.

International Impact

However, sometimes an artist's work becomes truly historical. Writer **David Morrell** remembers the moment he realized the true impact of his creation, Rambo:

I was once on a book tour in Poland. I was surprised how many people came to bookstores to meet me. Journalists lined up for three days for fifteen-minute interviews each. I finally said to one of them, "Why are you so interested in what I write?" She was a newspaper reporter who spoke English well. She said, "You need to understand the position of Rambo in Polish culture and the Solidarity movement." She told me that, in 1989, when Poland was about to break away from the Soviet Union, Rambo movies were illegal in Poland. Videotapes were smuggled in, and she was one of many who watched the movies in secret. She and her friends would have been punished if they were discovered watching them. After watching the movies, she and her friends and many, many others in other cities dressed as Rambo and used him as their motivation to demonstrate against the troops. She said to me, "In a way, Rambo helped to destroy the Soviet Union." When the Berlin Wall was being torn down, somebody wrote the word "Rambo" across it, as if Rambo had helped bring down the wall. In the United States, during the Vietnam War, people who hated the war blamed returning military personnel and spat on them and called them baby killers. When the film of *First Blood* came out in 1982 and Rambo talked about that, I think it helped Americans differentiate military personnel from politicians in terms of unpopular wars. You don't find anyone spitting on military personnel coming back from Iraq and Afghanistan, no matter how people might fiercely disagree with the politicians who declared those wars. In those cases, I think *First Blood* made a difference. Not many novels and films have done that.

However, when it comes to down to it, creativity can be the essence of who we are and what we leave behind – whether we change the world or only impact a single person. Writer-performance artist **Annie Lanzillotto** told us:

I think creativity is in every act of life. I think it's in every media, in the way you walk, the way you talk, the way you interact with people. One of the primary questions that I've pursued over the years is why did human beings want to mark the walls of caves? Why do dogs want to scratch the door? What's this impulse to mark your environment? From graffiti to hieroglyph-ics to writing on a computer or in the dirt as a kid, I think it's all creative. When I was nineteen, I climbed to the top of the pyramids in Giza, and got naked and there was graffiti from every era, with dates. Napoleon's army was up there; they graffitied their names. There's this impulse to mark your name. That's part of the creative impulse. The trees give their seeds and nuts. Even death is creativity; your bones go back into the dirt and your ashes go somewhere. The energy's got to go somewhere. My grandmother, when she died, she became a peach tree. It appeared after she died. It was where she used to spit her peach pits. To me, it was a manifestation of her energy. Now grandma's a peach tree. I think a lot about the cycles of legacy – where you leave your money to or where you leave your legacy, to your children or wherever. That's creative legacy. That's how you live. Just the act of turning on the fire and cooking. You're making. The act of making gives life.

References

Acar, S., Tadik, H., Uysal, R., Myers, D., & Inetas, B. (2023). Socio-economic status and creativity: A meta-analysis. *The Journal of Creative Behavior, 57*(1), 138–172.

Baer, J. (2022). *There's No Such Thing as Creativity: How Plato and 20th Century Psychology Have Misled Us.* New York: Cambridge University Press.

Baer, J., & Kaufman, J. C. (2017). The Amusement Park Theoretical Model of Creativity: An attempt to bridge the domain specificity/generality gap. In J. C. Kaufman, V. P. Glaveanu, & J. Baer (Eds.), *Cambridge Handbook of Creativity across Domains* (pp. 8–17). New York: Cambridge University Press.

(2005). Bridging generality and specificity: The Amusement Park Theoretical (APT) Model of Creativity. *Roeper Review, 27,* 158–163.

Barbot, B. (2018). "Generic" creativity as a predictor or outcome of identity development? *Creativity: Theories–Research–Applications, 5,* 159–164.

Beghetto, R. A., & Kaufman, J. C. (2007). Toward a broader conception of creativity: A case for "mini-c" creativity. *Psychology of Aesthetics, Creativity, and the Arts, 1,* 73–79.

Charland, W. (2010). African American youth and the artist's identity: Cultural models and aspirational foreclosure. *Studies in Art Education, 51*(2), 115–133.

Chen, Q., Beaty, R. E., & Qiu, J. (2020). Mapping the artistic brain: Common and distinct neural activations associated with musical, drawing, and literary creativity. *Human Brain Mapping, 41*(12), 3403–3419.

Csikszentmihalyi, M. (1996). *Creativity: Flow and the Psychology of Discovery and Invention.* New York: HarperCollins.

Dweck, C. S. (1986). Motivational processes affecting learning. *American Psychologist, 41,* 1040–1048.

(2000). *Self-Theories: Their Role in Motivation, Personality and Development.* Philadelphia: Taylor & Francis.

Ericsson, K. A., Roring, R. W., & Nandagopal, K. (2007). Giftedness and evidence for reproducibly superior performance: An account based on the expert-performance framework. *High Ability Studies, 18,* 3–56.

Gregerson, M., Snyder, H., & Kaufman, J. C. (Eds.) (2013). *Teaching Creatively and Teaching Creativity*. Dordrecht: Springer Science & Business Media.

Harwell, K., & Southwick, D. (2021). Beyond 10,000 hours: Addressing misconceptions of the expert performance approach. *Journal of Expertise*, 4, 2.

Kapoor, H., & Kaufman, J. C. (2020). Meaning-making through creativity during COVID-19. *Frontiers in Psychology*, 11, 595990.

Kapoor, H., Gurjar, S., Mahadeshwar, H., Rezaei, S., & Kaufman, J. C. (2024). Who is the most creative of them all? Art bias in laypersons' explicit and implicit beliefs. *Psychology of Aesthetics, Creativity, and the Arts*. Advance online publication. https://doi.org/10.1037/aca0000663.

Karwowski, M. (2021). School does not kill creativity. *European Psychologist*, 27(3), 263–275.

Katz, J. H., Mann, T. C., Shen, X., Goncalo, J. A., & Ferguson, M. J. (2022). Implicit impressions of creative people: Creativity evaluation in a stigmatized domain. *Organizational Behavior and Human Decision Processes*, 169, 104116.

Kaufman, J. C. (2023). *The Creativity Advantage*. New York: Cambridge University Press.

(2018). Finding meaning with creativity in the past, present, and future. *Perspectives on Psychological Science*, 13, 734–749.

Kaufman, J. C., & Baer, J. (2002). Could Steven Spielberg manage the Yankees?: Creative thinking in different domains. *Korean Journal of Thinking & Problem Solving*, 12, 5–15.

Kaufman, J. C., & Beghetto, R. A. (2009). Beyond big and little: The Four C Model of creativity. *Review of General Psychology*, 13, 1–12.

(2023). Where is the when of creativity? Specifying the temporal dimension of the Four Cs of creativity. *Review of General Psychology*, 27(2), 194–205.

Kostroff, M. (2019). *Audition Psych 101: A Refreshing Approach to the Dreaded Process*. Tampa, FL: Gatekeeper Press.

Kostroff, M., & Garnye, J. (2022). *The Stage Actor's Handbook*. Lanham, MD: Rowman & Littlefield.

Lee, Y. S., Chang, J. Y., & Choi, J. N. (2017). Why reject creative ideas? Fear as a driver of implicit bias against creativity. *Creativity Research Journal*, 29(3), 225–235.

Leibson, B. (2004). *I'm Too Young to Have Breast Cancer!* Washington, DC: LifeLine Press.

Lifton, R. J. (1979). *The Broken Connection*. New York: Simon & Schuster.

(2011). *Witness to an Extreme Century: A Memoir*. New York: Free Press.

Martela, F., & Steger, M. F. (2016). The three meanings of meaning in life: Distinguishing coherence, purpose, and significance. *The Journal of Positive Psychology, 11*(5), 531–545.

Mueller, J. S., Melwani, S., & Goncalo, J. A. (2012). The bias against creativity: Why people desire but reject creative ideas. *Psychological Science, 23*(1), 13–17.

Patston, T. J., Cropley, D. H., Marrone, R. L., & Kaufman, J. C. (2018). Teacher implicit beliefs of creativity: Is there an arts bias? *Teaching and Teacher Education, 75*, 366–374.

Penny, L. (2008). The highest of all the arts: Kant and poetry. *Philosophy and Literature, 32*(2), 373–384.

Perry, S. K. (1999). *Writing in Flow*. Cincinnati, OH: Writer's Digest Books.

Qian, M., Plucker, J. A., & Yang, X. (2019). Is creativity domain specific or domain general? Evidence from multilevel explanatory item response theory models. *Thinking Skills and Creativity, 33*, 100571.

Sanchez, M. (2023, November 5). How many hours do we spend in school? *Save Our Schools*. www.saveourschoolsmarch.org/how-many-hours-do-we-spend-in-school/

Simonton, D. K. (2014). Creative performance, expertise acquisition, individual differences, and developmental antecedents: An integrative research agenda. *Intelligence, 45*, 66–73.

(2009). *Genius 101*. New York: Springer.

Slayton, M. A, Bristol, A. S., & Viskontas, I. V. (2019). Factors affecting group creativity: Lessons from musical ensembles. *Current Opinion in Behavioral Sciences, 27*, 169–174.

Slayton, M. A., Romero-Sosa, J. L., Shore, K., Buonomano, D. V., & Viskontas, I. V. (2020). Musical expertise generalizes to superior temporal scaling in a Morse code tapping task. *PLOS One, 15*(1), e0221000.

Sternberg, R. J., Kaufman, J. C., & Pretz, J. E. (2002). *The Creativity Conundrum*. Philadelphia: Psychology Press.

Viskontas, I. (2019). *How Music Can Make You Better*. San Francisco: Chronicle Books.

Index

For EU product safety concerns, contact us at Calle de José Abascal, 56–1°,
28003 Madrid, Spain or eugpsr@cambridge.org.